AXIOM

First Principles of AI-Driven Software Development

Tony Adesanwo

CONTENTS

4 SIGNAL OVER NOISE

PART III: PROMPTING

5 PROMPT AS INTERFACE

6 COMPOSABILITY OVER COMPLEXITY

PART IV: AGENTS

7 SCOPE BEFORE AUTONOMY

8 HUMAN IN THE LOOP

PART V: EVAL

9 EVAL-FIRST DEVELOPMENT

10 GRACEFUL DEGRADATION

PART VI: FUTURE

11 ABSTRACT OVER THE MODEL LAYER

12 BUILD FOR DRIFT

Why First Principles, Why Now

The Speed Problem

In March 2023, GPT-4 launched and every product team in tech rewrote their roadmap within the week. Six months later, half of those roadmaps were already obsolete. Not because the teams were incompetent, but because the ground kept moving. New models, new capabilities, new pricing tiers, new open-source alternatives that performed at 80 percent of the frontier for a fraction of the cost. The cycle has not slowed down since. If anything, it has accelerated.

This is the defining condition of building software with AI: the tools change faster than the time it takes to learn them properly. A tutorial written in January is outdated by April. A framework that dominated in Q1 gets forked or replaced by Q3. The model you built your entire product around announces deprecation with 90 days notice. A new reasoning capability drops, and suddenly the architecture you spent three months designing around a known limitation no longer needs that workaround at all.

For most of software engineering history, this was not how things worked. Languages were stable for decades. Frameworks lasted years. The database you chose in 2010 was almost certainly the same database you were still running in 2020, and the skills you built around it transferred neatly to each new version. You could invest deeply in a stack and expect it to pay dividends over a long career horizon. There was always change, of course, but it was evolutionary. You had time to absorb it. You could plan around it.

The shift to AI-driven development broke that contract. And the instinct most teams have is to run faster: read more papers, attend more conferences, ship more prototypes, chase every new release. Keep up or get left behind. It feels productive. It looks like diligence.

It is also a trap.

Running faster works when the path is clear and the destination is fixed. When the terrain keeps shifting, speed without direction just means you cover more ground going nowhere useful. I have watched teams burn entire quarters rewriting prompt pipelines to accommodate a new model, only to discover that the model after that required a different approach entirely. I have seen startups raise funding on a technical advantage that evaporated within months because the capability they built around became a default feature of the next model release. I have seen engineering organizations adopt an "AI-first" strategy without any shared framework for what that actually means in practice, resulting in a dozen teams all making different and contradictory architectural decisions.

The common thread in these stories is not a lack of effort or talent. It is a lack of foundation. These teams were building on specifics, on particular models, particular frameworks, particular capabilities, without asking which of those specifics were load-bearing and which were incidental. When the incidental parts changed, they adapted fine. When the load-bearing parts changed, they scrambled.

What you need is not more speed. What you need is a way to evaluate new developments quickly, make sound architectural decisions under uncertainty, and build systems that do not collapse when the layer beneath them changes. You need a way of thinking about AI-driven software that stays relevant regardless of what gets released next week, next quarter, or next year.

That way of thinking is what this book is about. Not which model to use. Not which framework to adopt. The underlying logic of how good AI-driven systems are designed, tested, and sustained over time. A foundation that holds even when everything built on top of it needs to shift.

What First Principles Actually Mean

First principles thinking gets referenced constantly in tech, usually in a way that makes it sound more complicated than it is. Founders name-drop it in pitch decks. Engineering blogs invoke it to justify whatever decision they were going to make anyway. It has become shorthand for "I thought hard about this," which is not what the term actually means. So let me be direct about what I mean when I use it, because in this book it is not a rhetorical flourish. It is the structural foundation for every chapter that follows.

A first principle is a foundational claim that does not depend on any other claim for its validity. It is true on its own terms. You do not need to appeal to a framework, a vendor, a specific model, or a particular moment in time to justify it. In physics, these are things like conservation of energy. In software engineering, they are ideas like separation of concerns, the value of tight feedback loops, or the observation that complexity should be managed, not ignored. These are not rules handed down from authority. They are observations that have survived contact with reality across enough different contexts that they have earned a kind of structural trust.

The key property of a first principle is durability. It does not expire when a new tool comes out. It does not depend on a specific vendor's continued existence. It describes how a class of systems behaves, not which specific product to use this quarter. That durability is what makes first principles valuable in a landscape that changes as fast as AI does. They are the slowest-moving layer in your entire decision-making stack.

The 12 principles in this book operate at that level. They are not opinions about which model to use or which framework to adopt. They are claims about how AI-driven systems behave: what makes them reliable, what makes them fragile, and what patterns hold up regardless of the specific technology underneath.

Consider a few of them:

The model is not the product. This is true whether you are using GPT-4, Claude, Llama, Gemini, Mistral, or something released after this book goes to print. The principle holds because it describes a structural relationship between infrastructure and product value that does not depend on any particular model. The model is a capability. The product is what you build around that capability: the experience, the workflow, the integration, the data pipeline, the interface. Confusing the two is the single most common strategic mistake teams make, and it leads directly to fragile architecture, thin competitive moats, and panic every time a provider changes pricing or deprecates a version.

Context is architecture. The way you structure, curate, and inject context into a model determines the quality of its output more than almost any other variable you control. This was true with 4K token windows, it is true with 200K windows, and it will be true with whatever window size comes next. The specific techniques for managing context will evolve. The principle that context management is a first-class engineering discipline, on par with database schema design or API architecture, will not. If anything, it becomes more important as context windows grow, because having more space to fill means having more opportunity to fill it badly.

Autonomy is earned, not assumed. Every team building agentic systems eventually learns this lesson. The question is whether they learn it through careful, incremental scoping or through a production incident that takes down a workflow, corrupts data, or costs real money. The principle does not tell you how much autonomy to give your agent. It tells you that the answer should always be less than your first instinct, and that you should expand it incrementally based on evidence and observation, not ambition or optimism.

These are not tips. They are not best practices that expire with the next model release. They are structural observations about how AI systems work. And when you internalize them, they give you something that no tutorial or framework can: the ability to evaluate new developments on your own terms, make architectural decisions with confidence, and build systems that are designed to adapt rather than designed to be rewritten.

That is what first principles thinking actually gives you. Not answers to every question you will face. A reliable method for reasoning your way to good answers, even for questions that nobody has asked yet.

Who This Book Is For

This book is written for software engineers and technical leaders who are building products and systems that use AI. Not researchers trying to push the frontier of what models can do. Not people training their own foundation models from scratch. Practitioners. People who are making decisions every week about how to integrate language models, agent frameworks, and AI-driven features into real applications that real users depend on.

If you are a backend engineer trying to figure out how to structure your system around an LLM so that it is maintainable and testable, this book is for you. If you are a frontend engineer designing interfaces that surface AI output and need to handle the inherent uncertainty of that output gracefully, this book is for you. If you are a tech lead deciding whether to go agentic or keep a human in the loop, or trying to figure out how to evaluate whether your AI features are actually working, this book is for you. If you are an engineering manager trying to assess whether your team is building something durable or something that will need to be rewritten the next time a model gets deprecated, this book is for you.

I assume you know how to write software. I do not assume you have deep experience with machine learning or that you have been building AI products since the early GPT-3 era. What I assume is that you are practical, that you want to make good decisions, and that you would rather understand the reasoning behind a recommendation than just follow it blindly. If you are the kind of engineer who asks "why" before "how," you will find this book useful.

One thing this book deliberately avoids: hype. There is no shortage of books, blog posts, and conference talks telling you that AI changes everything, that the future is here, that we are on the verge of some transformative breakthrough every other month. Some of that is true. Most of it is not useful for the person who has to ship working software on a deadline and will be held accountable if it breaks.

What is useful is knowing, concretely, how to design a system that uses AI well. How to structure your prompts so they are maintainable and testable, not just clever. How to build context pipelines that improve output quality instead of drowning the model in noise. How to set up evaluation loops that actually tell you whether things are getting better or worse. How to scope an agent so it does useful work without running off the rails. How to build fallback paths so your system degrades gracefully instead of failing silently. How to make decisions about abstraction and provider independence that will still look smart twelve months from now.

That is the gap this book fills. Not the vision of what AI could become someday. The engineering of what it is right now, and how to build on it well.

A note for those coming from a data science or ML background: you will find some of this material familiar in concept but different in framing. This book approaches AI from the software engineering side, not the modeling side. The concerns are architectural: how do you integrate a probabilistic component into a system that users expect to behave reliably? How do you test something that gives slightly different answers each time? How do you build organizational practices around a technology that changes quarterly? If you already know how models work under the hood, this book will sharpen how you think about the systems built on top of them.

How the 12 Principles Connect

The principles in this book are not a grab bag of unrelated advice. They follow a deliberate sequence that mirrors how AI-driven systems get built in practice, and more importantly, how decisions at each layer cascade into the layers that follow.

Part I: Foundations starts with two principles that reframe how you think about AI before you write a line of code. Chapter 1 argues that the model is infrastructure, not product, and that your competitive edge lives in what you build around it. Chapter 2 tackles the mental shift from deterministic to probabilistic thinking, a shift that is easy to understand intellectually and surprisingly hard to internalize in practice. These two chapters set the conceptual ground for everything else. Get them wrong, and every downstream decision is built on sand.

Part II: Context moves into the architectural core of AI systems. Chapter 3 treats the context window as a first-class architectural surface. This is where most of your engineering leverage actually lives: not in the model you chose, but in what you feed it. Chapter 4 introduces signal-over-noise as a discipline: the idea that more context is not better context, and that ruthless curation of what goes into the model is one of the highest-leverage engineering activities you can perform. Together, these two chapters address the single biggest determinant of output quality in production systems.

Part III: Prompting addresses the interface layer between your intent and the model's output. Chapter 5 positions the prompt as an interface, subject to the same design discipline you would apply to any API contract: documented, versioned, tested against edge cases. Chapter 6 makes the case for composability: breaking complex prompt logic into focused, modular units that are easier to test, debug, and evolve independently. Monolithic prompts are the spaghetti code of AI systems, and this chapter shows you the alternative.

Part IV: Agents is about systems that act autonomously. Chapter 7 argues for scoping autonomy before granting it. Every agentic system needs clear, explicit boundaries around what it can and cannot do, defined upfront rather than discovered after something goes wrong in production. Chapter 8 addresses the human-in-the-loop question: where humans belong in an automated workflow, how to design those handoffs intentionally so they are useful rather than performative, and why full automation is often not the right goal.

Part V: Eval covers measurement and resilience. Chapter 9 introduces eval-first development: defining what good looks like before you build, then constructing the measurement infrastructure alongside the system itself. Without this discipline, you are flying blind, optimizing based on vibes instead of data. Chapter 10 addresses graceful degradation: the reality that AI systems fail in ways traditional software does not, and that your system needs explicit, designed plans for those moments rather than just hopes that they will not happen.

Part VI: Future closes the book with two chapters that share a single argument about change. Chapter 11 addresses the architectural response: abstracting over the model layer so your system is not welded to any single provider or model version. Chapter 12 addresses the human and organizational response: building team cultures, processes, and engineering habits designed to absorb what comes next rather than being disrupted by it. Together they argue that adaptability is not a feature you bolt on after launch. It is a core property of the system, designed in from the start.

The sequence matters because the dependencies are real. Foundations inform how you think about context. Context informs how you design prompts. Prompting informs how you scope agents. Agents create the need for evaluation. Evaluation and degradation patterns prepare you for change. And the final chapters on abstraction and drift close the loop by connecting back to the foundational claim: build on principles, not on specific implementations.

> *The progression mirrors the order in which decisions compound. A mistake in how you think about the model (Part I) will cascade into how you structure context (Part II), which will degrade your prompts (Part III), which will make your agents unreliable (Part IV), which will make them harder to evaluate (Part V), and which will make migration painful when the landscape shifts (Part VI). The principles build on each other because the systems they describe do too.*

How to Read This Book

You can read this book front to back. The sequence is designed for it, and if you are building your first AI-driven system or rethinking the architecture of an existing one, that is probably the best approach. The principles build on each other and reading them in order gives you the clearest picture of how they connect and reinforce one another.

But you can also use it as a reference. Each chapter is self-contained enough to be useful on its own. If you are in the middle of debugging a retrieval pipeline that keeps returning irrelevant results, go to Chapter 4. If you are about to deploy an agent and need to think through scope and permissions, Chapter 7. If your team just shipped an AI feature and realized they have no way to measure whether it is actually working well, start with Chapter 9. If you are worried about being locked into a single model provider and want to understand the architectural options, Chapter 11 addresses that directly.

Every chapter follows the same structure. It opens with the principle, stated clearly and without hedging. Then it builds the case for why the principle matters, using concrete engineering scenarios rather than abstract reasoning. Each chapter includes practical patterns you can apply immediately, trade-offs you should be aware of before making decisions, and common failure modes you should plan for rather than discover the hard way. And each chapter closes with a set of engineering heuristics: short, testable statements you can apply directly to your own systems. Think of the heuristics as the operational takeaway. They are designed to be specific enough to act on and general enough to survive the next model release.

I have tried to keep the chapters lean. I would rather give you 5,000 focused words that you actually internalize and apply than 15,000 words that cover every edge case but sit unread. If a chapter leaves you wanting more depth on a specific topic, that is by design. The goal is to give you the principle and enough practical grounding to use it well. Not to write the last word on every subject it touches.

A Word on the Examples

The examples in this book are drawn from real engineering scenarios. Some are from systems I have built or contributed to directly. Others are composites, assembled from patterns I have seen repeat across teams and organizations of different sizes, in different industries, facing different constraints. I have changed names, details, and specifics where necessary, but the engineering problems underneath are real. None of them are fabricated to make a theoretical point land neatly. If an example feels familiar, it is probably because you have encountered a version of the same problem yourself.

Where I use code, I keep it minimal and language-agnostic where possible. This book is not a cookbook.

If you need step-by-step implementation guides for a specific framework or language, there are better and more current resources for that. What this book gives you is the reasoning that should inform those implementations. The principle behind the pattern, not just the pattern itself. A good principle will help you write better code in any language. A code snippet divorced from principle will help you solve exactly one problem, exactly one time.

You will also notice that I do not name specific models or providers as recommendations. This is intentional, and it connects directly to the core thesis of the book. The moment I write "use Model X for this task," the advice starts a countdown clock. What I do instead is describe the capability you need and the criteria for selecting the right tool to deliver it. That way, whether you are reading this in 2025 or 2028, the reasoning still applies even if the specific model landscape looks completely different from when I wrote this.

There is one exception to this pattern: where a specific model, tool, or production incident illustrates a broader point about the industry or about a failure mode worth studying, I name it. History is useful for learning. Endorsements are not useful for a book that is supposed to last.

One more note on the examples: they are weighted toward the kinds of decisions that have the most downstream impact. You will see more about context architecture than about CSS for AI chatbots. More about evaluation design than about deploying a model to a specific cloud provider. The examples focus where the leverage is highest, because that is where getting it right matters most and where getting it wrong is most expensive to fix later.

The Case for Bedrock

This book exists because I kept seeing the same mistakes made by smart, capable engineers. Not because they lacked skill or effort, but because they lacked a framework for thinking about a category of software that does not behave like anything they built before. AI-driven systems are probabilistic, context-dependent, and built on infrastructure that changes constantly. The engineering instincts that work beautifully for deterministic systems, instincts around testing, reliability, architecture, and deployment, can actively mislead you when applied without adaptation to the AI domain.

Consider the instinct to write precise unit tests with exact expected outputs. In traditional software, this is good engineering. In AI systems, it leads to brittle test suites that break every time the model updates, even when the output quality has not degraded. The instinct is right in one context and wrong in another. Without a framework for understanding why, engineers end up either over-testing in ways that create busywork or under-testing in ways that let real regressions slip through. Chapter 9 addresses this directly, but the point here is broader: AI engineering requires you to re-examine instincts, not just acquire new tools.

Or consider the instinct to centralize logic. In traditional systems, a single function that handles all input processing is often the clean, maintainable choice. In AI systems, a single monolithic prompt that tries to handle every case is almost always the fragile choice. Composability, breaking things into smaller, focused pieces that can be tested and evolved independently, is not just a nice pattern. It is a structural requirement for systems that need to change frequently. Chapter 6 covers this in depth, but again, the underlying point is that your existing instincts need to be filtered through a new set of principles, not abandoned, but adapted.

The 12 principles in this book are my answer to that adaptation. They are not the only way to think about AI engineering, and I do not claim they are exhaustive. But they are grounded in how these systems actually behave in production, tested against real-world failure modes, and designed to stay useful regardless of which models, frameworks, or providers dominate the headlines next quarter. They are first principles because they describe structural properties of the systems, not transient features of the tools.

If you take one thing from this introduction, let it be this: the teams that build the best AI products over the next decade will not be the ones who adopted the right model at the right time. They will be the ones who learned to reason clearly about a class of problems that did not exist five years ago, and who built that reasoning into their architecture, their processes, and their engineering culture. The right model at the right time is luck. Clear reasoning about system design is a skill. Skills compound. Luck does not.

That reasoning starts with principles. And this is where those principles are laid out.

Let us get started.

The Model is Not the Product

Part I: Foundations

Most teams building with AI make the same foundational mistake: they treat the model as the end. The product is the experience, the workflow, the outcome you create on top of it. What you build around the model is what defines your competitive edge.

The Infrastructure Framing

When electricity first became available for commercial use, companies did not sell electricity as a product. They sold what electricity made possible: light, manufacturing capacity, refrigeration, communication. The companies that thrived were not the ones with the best generators. They were the ones that understood what to build on top of a new kind of power.

AI models are in a similar position today. They are extraordinarily powerful, general-purpose capabilities. But a capability is not a product. A product solves a specific problem for a specific user in a specific context. The model does not do that on its own. The model gives you the raw material. Everything that turns that raw material into something a user actually wants, the interface, the data pipeline, the workflow integration, the guardrails, the evaluation loops, the domain-specific logic, that is the product.

This distinction sounds obvious when stated plainly, but it is violated constantly in practice. Go to any startup pitch competition focused on AI and count how many pitches start with which model they use. Look at product landing pages that lead with the model name in their headline. Watch how engineering teams make architectural decisions based on the assumption that the model they chose today is the model they will be using in a year. Listen to how roadmap discussions start with "what can the model do now?" rather than "what does the user need?" All of these are symptoms of the same confusion: treating the model as the product instead of treating it as the infrastructure the product runs on.

The confusion is understandable. In traditional software, infrastructure is boring. Databases, servers, message queues, these are important but they do not capture anyone's imagination. AI models are different. They produce visible, impressive, sometimes surprising outputs. They can write, reason, summarize, translate, code, and generate content that was previously the exclusive domain of human expertise. It is natural to look at that and think: the model is the product. The model is what makes this special.

But "special" and "product" are not the same thing. The model is what makes the category possible. Your product is what makes your specific offering valuable. Those are two very different things, and conflating them leads to architectural decisions you will regret.

Infrastructure is replaceable by definition. That is not a weakness; it is a design property. You do not build your business strategy around a specific database version. You do not pitch investors on which cloud provider hosts your servers. You use the best infrastructure available for your needs, and you build your actual value on top of it. AI models deserve the same framing.

The resistance to this framing usually comes from the fact that AI models feel different from other infrastructure. A database does not generate creative text. A cloud server does not reason about your user's intent. The capability surface of an AI model is so broad and so impressive that it naturally draws attention to itself. But that is exactly the trap. The more impressive the infrastructure, the more tempting it is to confuse the infrastructure with the product. And the more painful that confusion becomes when the infrastructure changes.

I have seen this play out in a predictable pattern. A team discovers a new model capability, something it could not do before or could not do reliably. They build a feature around it. The feature works, users love it, and the team celebrates. Then, six months later, the model updates and the behavior changes subtly. Not broken, exactly, but different. The output format shifts. The tone drifts. Confidence levels on edge cases change. The team scrambles to adapt, because they built directly on a specific model behavior instead of building on an abstraction layer that could accommodate variation. The fix is always the same: add the product layer they should have built from the beginning. The cost of adding it after the fact is always higher than building it upfront.

When you adopt the infrastructure framing, it changes the questions you ask. Instead of "which model should we use?" the question becomes "what are we building that needs a model, and what does that model need to be good at?" Instead of "how do we get the most out of GPT-4?" the question becomes "what experience are we delivering to the user, and which model best supports that experience right now?" The shift is subtle but it reorients your entire engineering strategy around value you control rather than capabilities you rent.

Model vs. Product Layer

Every AI-driven application has, whether the team recognizes it or not, two distinct layers. There is the model layer, which handles inference: you send it input, it returns output. And there is the product layer, which handles everything else: what input to send, how to prepare it, what to do with the output, how to present it, how to handle failure, how to improve over time.

The model layer is, increasingly, a commodity. Not in the sense that all models are identical, they are not, but in the sense that multiple providers offer models capable of handling the same categories of tasks at roughly comparable quality levels. The gap between the best model and the fifth-best model for most production use cases is smaller than most people assume, and it is shrinking with every release cycle. This means that any advantage you gain from choosing the right model is temporary. Someone else has access to the same model, or a comparable one, or will have access to one soon enough.

This is a hard truth for engineering teams that invested significant time evaluating and selecting their model. It feels like that selection should matter more. And in fairness, model selection does matter for specific tasks, especially at the margins. If your use case requires exceptional performance on a narrow capability, like complex mathematical reasoning or low-resource language translation, the difference between models can be significant. But for the vast majority of production AI features, the model is necessary but not sufficient. It is the floor, not the ceiling.

The product layer is the ceiling. It is where durable value lives. Consider what goes into it:

Context engineering. How you retrieve, structure, and inject relevant information into the model. A well-designed RAG pipeline that surfaces the right documents with the right chunking strategy and the right ranking is worth more than any model upgrade. The model processes what you give it. The quality of what you give it is your engineering problem, and your competitive advantage.

Prompt architecture. How you translate user intent into model instructions. A carefully designed prompt system with version control, edge case handling, and output specifications is an asset that transfers across models. A collection of ad hoc prompts copy-pasted from ChatGPT threads is a liability.

Workflow integration. How the AI component fits into the user's actual working process. An AI feature that meets users where they already work, inside their existing tools, in the flow of their existing tasks, with minimal friction, delivers more value than a technically superior feature that requires users to change their behavior.

Evaluation infrastructure. How you measure whether your AI features are actually working well. Teams that build robust eval pipelines, with golden datasets, automated scoring, and regression detection, can iterate faster and with more confidence than teams flying on user complaints and gut feelings.

Guardrails and fallbacks. How your system handles the inevitable cases where the model gets it wrong. A thoughtful degradation strategy that routes low-confidence responses to a human reviewer, surfaces uncertainty to the user, or falls back to a simpler but more reliable path, that is product engineering. The model itself does not provide this. You do.

None of these are model-specific. Every one of them can be designed, built, and refined independently of which model sits underneath. And every one of them represents work that your competitors have to do for themselves, regardless of which model they use. That is what makes them durable. That is what makes them yours.

There is a useful mental model here. Think of the model layer as rented capability and the product layer as owned capability. Rented capability is powerful but shared. You get access to it through an API key, and so does everyone else. It can be repriced, deprecated, or outperformed at any time, and you have no control over when that happens. Owned capability is everything you build on top: the domain logic, the data pipelines, the user insights, the evaluation frameworks, the workflow integrations. Rented capability gets you started. Owned capability is what lets you stay.

The best AI products I have worked with have a thick product layer and a thin model layer. The model is one component, important but interchangeable. The product layer is deep, specific, and hard to replicate. Getting to that ratio is not accidental. It requires deliberate investment in the owned side, starting from day one, not as a later optimization.

The investment math here is worth making explicit. Most teams I have observed spend roughly 70 to 80 percent of their engineering time on the model layer in early development: experimenting with models, tuning prompts by trial and error, optimizing token usage, working around model-specific limitations. They spend 20 to 30 percent on the product layer: the context pipeline, the evaluation framework, the workflow integration, the failure handling. The teams that build durable products eventually invert this ratio. They get their model integration to a stable, abstracted state relatively quickly and then pour the majority of their effort into the product layer. The teams that never invert the ratio tend to stay on the treadmill, constantly reacting to model changes and never building the depth that would make those changes manageable. Recognize which phase your team is in, and plan your investment accordingly.

Why "GPT-Powered" Is Not a Strategy

In 2023 and 2024, a wave of startups launched with positioning that amounted to "we built a wrapper around GPT-4." Some of them were quite good. The interfaces were clean, the use cases were well-chosen, the execution was solid. But the positioning itself, leading with the model name, revealed a strategic vulnerability that many of those companies are now confronting.

When your differentiation is the model, you have no differentiation. Here is why.

First, model access is not exclusive. Every major model provider offers API access to anyone willing to pay. The model you built your product on is available to every competitor, every new entrant, every large company that decides to add your feature to their existing platform. You are competing on something that is, by design, available to everyone.

Second, model capabilities converge. Each generation of models from different providers gets closer in quality for most production tasks. A feature that was only possible with GPT-4 in early 2023 was achievable with Claude, Gemini, and several open-source models by late 2024. Leading with a specific model name ties your brand to a capability that will be table stakes within months.

Third, model naming creates a dependency in your users' minds. If your landing page says "powered by GPT-4," your users now associate your product's quality with that specific model. When GPT-5 launches, they expect you to upgrade immediately. When a competitor launches on GPT-5 first, they wonder why you have not. You have handed your users a benchmark that you do not control and that has nothing to do with the actual value your product delivers.

Fourth, and this is the one that catches teams off guard: the platform provider can become your competitor overnight. If you build a thin layer on top of a model and market yourself as a convenient way to access that model's capabilities, what happens when the model provider builds the same convenience directly into their own product? OpenAI ships ChatGPT features. Anthropic ships Claude features. Google ships Gemini features. Every one of them has the same model you have, plus the advantage of zero API latency and zero per-token cost. If your value proposition is "we made it easy to use Model X for Y task," you are one product update away from having the model provider do that for free.

The companies that survive and grow past this vulnerability are the ones that built something the model provider cannot replicate by adding a feature: deep domain expertise encoded into their product layer, proprietary data pipelines that improve with every customer interaction, workflow integrations that are specific to an industry or a job function, evaluation infrastructure tuned to a narrow and important use case. These are things that take months or years to build. They represent accumulated engineering and domain knowledge that does not come bundled with an API key.

The alternative is to build a brand and a product identity that is model-agnostic. Your product name, your feature descriptions, your marketing, your documentation, none of it should depend on a specific model for its meaning. Users should associate your product with the outcome it delivers, not the infrastructure it runs on. Nobody cares which database powers their favorite app. Over time, nobody will care which model powers their favorite AI tool either. They will care whether it works.

This does not mean you should hide which model you use. Transparency about your infrastructure is fine, even admirable. The point is that your strategy should not depend on it. If someone asked you to explain your competitive advantage, and the honest answer is "we use a good model," that is the moment to rethink your product layer. Because every one of your competitors can give the same answer.

There is a common objection here worth addressing directly: "But we are not just a wrapper. We have a great UX." I hear this frequently, and it deserves an honest response. A great UX is absolutely part of the product layer. But a great UX alone is a thin product layer. Interfaces can be replicated. Design patterns spread quickly. If your product layer consists of a polished interface on top of a raw model API, you are one well-funded competitor away from being outdesigned by a team that also has your model access plus more resources. UX is necessary but not sufficient. The durable parts of the product layer are the ones that involve accumulated domain knowledge, proprietary data loops, and engineering infrastructure that takes real time to build correctly. A beautiful interface is the visible part. The invisible parts are what make it defensible.

Another common objection: "We have fine-tuned the model for our specific use case." Fine-tuning is product-layer work, and it can be valuable. But it is also the most model-dependent investment you can make. A fine-tuned model is, by definition, coupled to a specific base model. If the base model gets deprecated or a better base model becomes available, your fine-tuning investment does not transfer. The training data and the methodology transfer, but the model itself does not. If fine-tuning is a core part of your strategy, make sure you are also investing in the parts that are portable: the training data curation, the evaluation methodology, the performance benchmarks. Those are the durable assets. The fine-tuned weights are temporary.

Building Durable Value

If the model is infrastructure and the product layer is where value lives, the natural question is: what specifically should you invest in to build something durable? Something that does not become worthless the next time a model gets upgraded or a provider changes pricing?

The answer comes down to a simple test: what survives a model swap?

Imagine that tomorrow, your model provider shuts down entirely, or raises prices by 10x, or gets surpassed by a competitor that offers better quality at half the cost. You need to swap to a different model within 30 days. What parts of your system carry over, and what parts do you have to rebuild from scratch?

This is not a hypothetical exercise. Model deprecations happen regularly. Pricing changes have forced companies to migrate under time pressure. New model releases have made previously expensive approaches affordable, which is good news, unless your architecture is too tightly coupled to take advantage of it. The swap scenario is not a question of if, but of when and how painful.

The parts that carry over are your actual product. The parts that do not were always borrowed.

Here is what typically survives a model swap: your domain knowledge about the problem space and your users. Your data pipelines and context retrieval infrastructure. Your prompt templates, assuming they are well-structured enough to port (which composable prompts are and monolithic prompts are not). Your evaluation datasets and scoring rubrics. Your UX patterns for handling uncertainty and failure. Your workflow integrations with other systems. Your understanding of which edge cases matter most and how frequently they occur.

Here is what typically does not survive: hardcoded model-specific parameters and quirks. Prompts that exploit specific model behaviors rather than clearly expressing intent. Token-level optimizations tied to a specific tokenizer. Fine-tuned versions of a specific base model. Pricing assumptions built around a specific provider's rate card. Retry and timeout logic calibrated to a specific provider's latency profile. Output parsing logic that depends on a specific model's formatting habits rather than enforcing structure through explicit output schemas.

There is a middle category that is worth noting: components that partially survive. System prompts, for example, usually carry over in intent but need adjustment in phrasing. A system prompt that works well with one model might need different emphasis or structure to achieve the same result with another. This is adaptation work, not rebuild work, and the distinction matters. If your system prompt is well-documented and its intent is clearly stated separately from its phrasing, the adaptation takes hours. If the prompt evolved through trial and error with no documentation about why specific phrasings were chosen, the adaptation can take weeks because you are essentially reverse-engineering your own design decisions.

The ratio between these two categories tells you how durable your system actually is. If 80 percent of your engineering work transfers cleanly to a new model and the remaining 20 percent is adaptation work, you are in good shape. If the ratio is reversed, you have built a system that is effectively leased from your model provider. You own the UX layer. They own everything that makes it work.

This is worth measuring concretely. Take an afternoon with your team and audit your codebase. Tag every module, every pipeline, every configuration file as either model-dependent or model-independent. You will likely be surprised at how much model-specific logic has crept into places where it does not need to be. A model name hardcoded in a service configuration. A prompt that uses phrasing optimized for one model's quirks. A retry strategy calibrated to one provider's rate limits. Each of these is a small coupling that is easy to add and tedious to remove later.

The teams I have seen navigate model transitions most successfully are the ones that treated model independence as a design constraint from the beginning. Not because they planned to switch, but because designing for portability forced them to be disciplined about where they put their engineering effort. It forced them to build robust context pipelines rather than relying on the model to figure out messy inputs. It forced them to write clear, intent-driven prompts rather than gaming specific model quirks. It forced them to invest in evaluation infrastructure rather than relying on manual spot checks. All of these investments made their system better on their current model, and they made the eventual model swap far less painful.

Durability is not about predicting the future. It is about building in a way that is structurally sound regardless of which future arrives.

There is a useful parallel to how experienced teams think about database migrations. Nobody enjoys migrating a database. But the teams that design their data layer with clean abstractions, good schema hygiene, and well-tested migration scripts handle it as a routine operation. The teams that embedded raw SQL queries throughout their application layer, or made assumptions about specific database behaviors in their business logic, treat every migration like a crisis. The same dynamic applies to model transitions. The pain of a model swap is directly proportional to how much model-specific logic you allowed to leak into your product layer. The principle is identical. Only the infrastructure is different.

Case Study: Two Apps, Same Model

Consider two companies, both building AI-powered contract review tools. Both use the same foundation model. Both launched within a few months of each other. Both target the same market: mid-size law firms that want to speed up due diligence.

Company A built a clean chat interface on top of the model's API. Users upload a contract, ask questions about it in natural language, and get answers. The engineering effort went primarily into the interface: a polished upload flow, a well-designed conversation view, fast response times. The prompts were relatively simple, along the lines of "You are a legal analyst. The user has uploaded the following contract. Answer their questions about it." The system worked well in demos. It looked impressive. Investors were enthusiastic. The entire product was built in about six weeks with a team of four.

Company B took a different approach. Before writing any interface code, they spent eight weeks interviewing paralegals and junior associates at law firms. They observed how contract review actually happens day to day, not the idealized version, but the messy, repetitive, high-stakes reality. They learned that contract review is not a question-and-answer process. It is a checklist process. Reviewers work through specific categories of risk: indemnification clauses, termination provisions, liability caps, assignment restrictions, governing law, change of control provisions, intellectual property rights. They are not asking open-ended questions. They are verifying that specific provisions exist, that they meet certain standards, and that there are no unusual deviations from standard terms. The output of a contract review is not a conversation. It is a structured report.

Company B built their product around this workflow. Instead of a chat interface, they built a structured review dashboard. When a user uploads a contract, the system runs a series of focused extraction and analysis prompts, each targeting a specific category of risk. The results populate a checklist view, with each item color-coded by confidence level. Items flagged as high-risk or low-confidence are surfaced for human review. The prompts are composable: each extraction task has its own focused prompt, its own output schema, and its own evaluation dataset. The context pipeline uses a custom chunking strategy optimized for legal document structure, splitting on clause boundaries rather than arbitrary token counts.

Company B also invested heavily in their data loop. Every time a human reviewer corrected a system output, that correction fed back into the evaluation dataset. After six months, they had thousands of annotated examples across dozens of contract types. This dataset was not model-specific. It encoded domain expertise about what good contract analysis looks like, and it could be used to evaluate any model's output against a ground truth. It was, in a real sense, the most valuable asset the company owned, and it was not something you could download or buy from a model provider.

Both products use the same model. But they are not in the same competitive position.

When the model provider released a new version with different behavioral characteristics, Company A had to spend weeks re-tuning their generic prompt to get equivalent output quality. Their simple prompt was sensitive to model changes precisely because it was simple: it relied on the model's defaults for everything. Company B ran their existing eval suite against the new model, identified two extraction tasks where quality had drifted, adjusted those specific prompts, and deployed the update in three days. Their composable architecture meant the change was isolated, testable, and low-risk.

When a competitor launched a similar product using a different, cheaper model, Company A had no structural defense. A chat interface on top of a model is something any team can replicate in a weekend. Company B had a defense that their competitor would need months to replicate: the structured review workflow, the domain-specific chunking strategy, the per-category evaluation datasets, the confidence-gated human review flow, the growing corpus of annotated corrections from real legal reviewers. None of that was model-specific. All of it was hard-won product engineering.

There is a useful detail in how Company B approached model selection that illustrates the infrastructure framing. When their engineering lead was asked which model they used, her answer was: "Whichever one scores highest on our eval suite this quarter." They had built their system so that swapping the model was a configuration change, not an architecture change. Their evaluation datasets, built from real contract reviews, were the source of truth. The model was the component being evaluated, not the foundation the system depended on. That inversion, making the model serve the product layer rather than the other way around, is exactly what the infrastructure framing looks like in practice.

The lesson is not that Company B was smarter or that Company A was doomed. Company A could still build these layers, and the best teams do course-correct once they see the vulnerability. The lesson is that the model gave both companies the same starting capability, and what they built around that capability determined everything that followed. The model was the common denominator. The product layer was the differentiator. It always is.

Engineering Heuristics

Each chapter in this book closes with a set of engineering heuristics: short, testable statements you can apply directly to your own systems. These are not abstract wisdom. They are operational checks. Use them in design reviews, in architecture discussions, in retrospectives after a feature ships. They are meant to be pinned somewhere visible and referenced often.

Heuristic 1: If your differentiator is the model, you have no differentiator.

This is the core test. If a competitor can replicate your product by using the same model and building a comparable interface in a few weeks, your product layer is too thin. Your competitive advantage should be something that takes months to build and is hard to copy: your domain knowledge encoded in your context pipelines, your evaluation infrastructure built from real user data, your workflow integrations that reflect deep understanding of how your users actually work. If the model is the most impressive thing about your product, the next model release will erase whatever head start you had. Apply this test honestly in your next product review. If the answer makes you uncomfortable, that discomfort is useful information.

Heuristic 2: Name your product layer separately from your model choice.

This is a practical exercise, not just a branding suggestion. Sit down with your team and list every component of your system. Then label each one: is this the model layer or the product layer? If you struggle to name product-layer components that are distinct from the model, that is a signal. You should be able to describe your context engineering, your prompt architecture, your evaluation strategy, and your workflow integration as independent, named subsystems with their own documentation, their own tests, and their own roadmaps. If you cannot, your product layer is probably underdeveloped and your system is more model-dependent than you realize.

Heuristic 3: Ask: what survives a model swap?

Run this thought experiment quarterly, ideally as part of a structured team exercise. Assume your current model disappears tomorrow and you have to migrate to an alternative within 30 days. What percentage of your codebase, your infrastructure, your institutional knowledge carries over? What percentage has to be rebuilt? Track this ratio over time. If the percentage of portable work is going up, you are investing in the right layer. If it is flat or declining, you are accumulating model-specific debt that will cost you during the next transition. And there will be a next transition. The teams that treat this exercise as routine, rather than as an emergency response, are the ones that handle transitions gracefully when they come.

The model is not the product. It is the most powerful piece of infrastructure you have ever had access to, and the appropriate response to powerful infrastructure is to build something extraordinary on top of it. Not to mistake it for the extraordinary thing itself.

This distinction will echo throughout every chapter that follows. When we discuss context architecture in Part II, we are discussing a product-layer discipline. When we discuss prompt design in Part III, we are discussing a product-layer interface. When we discuss evaluation in Part V, we are measuring product-layer quality. The model layer is present in all of these, but it is always the thing being used, never the thing being built. Keeping that relationship clear is the first principle because it shapes every principle that comes after it.

In the next chapter, we turn to the mental shift that makes all of this possible: learning to think probabilistically in a profession that has spent decades expecting determinism. If this chapter is about what AI is in your system, the next chapter is about how AI behaves, and why that behavior demands a fundamentally different approach to design and engineering.

Embrace Probabilistic Thinking

Part I: Foundations

Software engineers are trained to expect determinism. AI breaks that contract. Reliability in AI systems does not mean guaranteed correctness. It means consistent behavior across a distribution of inputs and conditions.

Determinism vs. Probability

If you have spent any meaningful time writing software, you carry a deep assumption that most engineers never even think to examine: given the same input, a system should produce the same output. This is determinism, and it is the bedrock of how traditional software is designed, tested, and trusted.

You write a function. You pass it an input. You get a result. You pass it the same input tomorrow, next week, next year. You get the same result. This property is so fundamental that the entire testing infrastructure of modern software depends on it. Unit tests, integration tests, regression tests, they all assert that a known input produces a known output. If that assertion fails, something is broken and needs to be fixed.

AI systems do not work this way.

Send the same prompt to the same model twice, and you may get two different responses. Not because something is broken. Because the system is probabilistic. It is sampling from a distribution of possible outputs, weighted by the model's learned patterns and whatever temperature setting you have configured. The responses will usually be similar in meaning and structure, but they will not be identical. The phrasing will differ. The level of detail may vary. The order of information might change. And in edge cases, the semantic content itself might diverge in ways that matter.

For engineers coming from deterministic systems, this feels like a bug. It feels like unreliability. And the instinct, the very reasonable instinct, is to try to eliminate it. Set the temperature to zero. Lock down the output format. Pin to a specific model version. Do whatever it takes to get the system to behave the way software is supposed to behave: predictably, repeatably, verifiably.

This instinct is understandable, but it is also counterproductive. Trying to force determinism onto a probabilistic system does not make the system deterministic. It makes you blind to the variance that still exists. A temperature of zero does not guarantee identical outputs across different model versions, different hardware, or even different API calls. It just narrows the distribution. You can pin to a model version, but model versions get deprecated. You can lock the output format, which is often wise, but the content within that format is still sampled.

The productive response is not to eliminate variance. It is to understand it, plan for it, and design your system around it. That requires a genuine shift in how you think about correctness, testing, and reliability. Not a minor adjustment. A different mental model.

Let me make the shift concrete with an example. Say you are building a feature that extracts key dates from contracts: effective date, termination date, renewal deadlines. In a deterministic system, you would write a parser, run it against test cases, and verify that each test case produces the exact expected output. If the parser returns the wrong date, there is a bug to fix. Once the bug is fixed, the test passes reliably, forever.

In a probabilistic system, the model might extract the correct dates 95 percent of the time. The other 5 percent might include cases where it misreads an ambiguous date format, confuses a renewal deadline with a notice period, or hallucinates a date that appears in a different section of the document. There is no single bug to fix. The failure is distributed across a range of inputs, and the fix is not a code change but a combination of better prompting, better context injection, confidence scoring, and validation logic. Your test does not assert a single expected output. It asserts that accuracy across a representative dataset remains above a defined threshold. And you run that test regularly, because the threshold can degrade without any code change on your part, simply because the model updated.

This is fundamentally different from how most engineers were trained to think about quality. It is not worse. It is not less rigorous. But it requires different tools, different instincts, and a willingness to embrace the reality that "correct" in a probabilistic system means "reliably within acceptable bounds" rather than "identical every time."

In deterministic software, correctness means: given input X, the system produces output Y. In probabilistic software, correctness means: given input X, the system produces an output that falls within an acceptable range of outputs, with a known frequency of failure modes that are handled gracefully. The shift from a single expected output to a distribution of acceptable outputs is the core conceptual change, and everything else in this chapter follows from it.

Designing for Distributions

Once you accept that your system's output is drawn from a distribution rather than a fixed point, the design question changes. Instead of asking "what will the system output?" you start asking "what is the range of things the system might output, and which parts of that range are acceptable?"

This is not a new concept in engineering generally. Civil engineers design bridges for a distribution of loads, not a single expected weight. Financial engineers model portfolios for a range of market conditions, not a single predicted outcome. Even traditional software handles distributions in certain contexts: network latency, user behavior patterns, load distribution across servers. What is new is applying this thinking to the core output of your system, the thing you are showing to your user or acting on in your workflow.

Designing for distributions means three things in practice.

First, you define what acceptable looks like before you look at actual outputs. This is harder than it sounds. For a summarization feature, what counts as an acceptable summary? Is it one that captures all key points? Most key points? The right key points for a specific audience? What about tone, length, reading level? You need to answer these questions explicitly, in writing, before you start evaluating model outputs. Otherwise you will find yourself constantly moving the goalposts, accepting whatever the model gives you when it looks reasonable and rejecting it when it does not, without any consistent standard.

Second, you characterize the actual distribution of outputs your system produces. Run your system against a representative set of inputs, not ten examples, but hundreds or thousands. Look at the results. Where does the system reliably produce acceptable output? Where does it occasionally miss? Where does it fail consistently? The answers will form a map of your system's reliability surface, and that map is far more useful than any single test result. You will find that most AI systems are remarkably good across a wide range of typical inputs and remarkably brittle on a narrower range of edge cases. Knowing exactly where those edges are is the difference between a system you can deploy with confidence and one you are hoping will work.

Third, you design different handling for different parts of the distribution. The high-confidence, clearly-acceptable outputs get routed directly to the user or the next step in the workflow. The low-confidence, borderline outputs get routed to a review step, a human check, or a fallback path. The clearly unacceptable outputs get caught and handled before they reach the user at all. This is not just error handling. It is the core architecture of a probabilistic system. The routing logic, the confidence thresholds, the fallback paths, these are first-class architectural components, not afterthoughts bolted on during QA.

The practical implication is that your system needs to know, at runtime, how confident it should be in its own output. This is not a feature you add later. It is a capability you design in from the beginning, because every downstream decision, what to show the user, whether to ask for confirmation, whether to trigger a human review, depends on it.

A useful exercise at this stage is to draw the distribution you expect for any given AI feature. On one axis, put output quality: unacceptable, marginal, acceptable, excellent. On the other, put frequency: how often does each quality level occur? You want a distribution that is heavily weighted toward acceptable and excellent, with a thin tail on the marginal and unacceptable ends. Your architecture should explicitly handle each zone. The goal is not to pretend the thin tail does not exist. It is to make sure your system behaves well across the entire curve.

Teams that skip this exercise tend to design for the center of the distribution and discover the tails in production. A user submits an input the team did not anticipate, the model produces output in the marginal zone, and the system passes it through as if it were excellent because there is no quality gate to distinguish the two. The user loses trust. The team scrambles to add handling after the fact. The fix is always more expensive when it is reactive than when it is designed in from the start.

Confidence Thresholds

The concept of a confidence threshold is simple: you define a numerical boundary that determines how your system handles a given output. Above the threshold, the output is treated as reliable and acted on automatically. Below the threshold, the output is flagged for additional handling. The concept is simple. Getting the threshold right is not.

Start with the question: what is the cost of being wrong?

If you are building a system that suggests email subject lines, the cost of a mediocre suggestion is low. The user sees it, decides it is not great, and types their own. You can afford a relatively low confidence threshold because the failure mode is mild and easily recoverable. The user barely notices.

If you are building a system that auto-applies labels to customer support tickets and routes them to different teams, the cost of a wrong label is higher. A misrouted ticket means delayed response time, frustrated customers, and wasted effort by the wrong team. You need a higher confidence threshold, and you need a clear path for tickets that fall below it, probably a manual triage queue.

If you are building a system that drafts medical summaries or legal recommendations, the cost of an incorrect output is severe. A wrong medical summary could affect treatment decisions. A wrong legal recommendation could expose a client to liability. The confidence threshold should be very high, and outputs below that threshold should not reach the end user without human review under any circumstances.

The mistake I see most often is not that teams set the wrong threshold. It is that they do not set one at all. The system produces output, the output goes to the user, and the implicit assumption is that the model is right often enough for it to be fine. This is not engineering. It is hoping. And it works right up until it does not, at which point the failure is often more expensive than building the confidence infrastructure would have been.

Implementing confidence thresholds in practice requires a way to score output confidence. There are several approaches, and they can be combined. The model itself can be asked to rate its confidence, though self-reported confidence should be calibrated against actual accuracy. You can use consistency checks, running the same prompt multiple times and measuring how much the outputs agree. You can compare the output against known patterns or schemas to verify structural correctness. You can use secondary models as judges, evaluating the primary model's output. None of these approaches are perfect on their own, but in combination they give you a workable signal.

The threshold itself should not be a fixed number decided once and never revisited. It should be a tunable parameter that you adjust based on observed performance. Start conservative, with a high threshold that routes more outputs to human review. As you gather data on actual accuracy at different confidence levels, adjust the threshold to find the right balance between automation and oversight for your specific use case. This is an iterative process, and it requires the evaluation infrastructure described in Chapter 9.

One practical pattern that works well: implement your confidence threshold as a configuration value that can be changed without a code deploy. Give your operations team or your product manager visibility into the confidence distribution, how many outputs fall above and below the threshold, and how accurate the above-threshold outputs actually are. This creates a feedback loop where the people closest to the outcomes can adjust the threshold based on real-world performance, rather than relying on an engineer's initial guess about what the right number should be.

A common mistake is to treat confidence as binary: the system is either confident or it is not. In practice, confidence is a spectrum, and your system should handle multiple zones on that spectrum differently. Consider three zones rather than two. High confidence outputs get processed automatically. Medium confidence outputs get processed but with a visible indicator to the user that the result should be verified. Low confidence outputs get routed to a human reviewer or a fallback path. The three-zone model is not the only option, but it captures a nuance that the binary approach misses, and it usually maps well to how users actually want to interact with AI-generated output.

When "Good Enough" Is the Right Goal

There is a cultural resistance in software engineering to the phrase "good enough." Engineers are trained to strive for correctness. Correct code. Correct outputs. Correct behavior. The idea of deliberately designing for "good enough" feels like cutting corners. It feels like accepting mediocrity.

In probabilistic systems, this instinct needs to be re-examined. Not abandoned. Re-examined.

Perfectionism in a deterministic system is achievable and worthwhile. You can write a sorting algorithm that is provably correct. You can build a payment processing pipeline where every transaction is guaranteed to be handled exactly once. The investment in correctness pays off because the system can actually deliver on that guarantee.

Perfectionism in a probabilistic system is not achievable in the same way, and pursuing it has real costs. You can spend months trying to get a summarization feature from 92 percent accuracy to 95 percent accuracy, and those three percentage points might require a complete rearchitecture of your context pipeline, a much more expensive model, or both. Meanwhile, the 92 percent version is already delivering real value to users who would rather have a mostly-accurate summary right now than a perfect summary never.

The engineering question is not "is this output perfect?" It is "is this output useful, and is the failure mode acceptable?" Those are different questions, and they lead to different design decisions.

Consider a feature that auto-generates commit messages based on a diff. If the generated message accurately captures the change 85 percent of the time, and the other 15 percent produces messages that are vague but not wrong, that is probably a good enough feature to ship. The cost of a vague commit message is low. The developer sees it, edits it in two seconds, and moves on. The time saved on the 85 percent of correct generations easily outweighs the minor inconvenience of the 15 percent that need editing.

Now consider a feature that auto-fills insurance claim forms. If the system gets the claim amount wrong 15 percent of the time, that is not good enough, regardless of how much time it saves on the other 85 percent. The cost of an incorrect claim amount is high enough that the failure rate needs to be much lower, or the system needs to flag those fields for mandatory human verification.

The "good enough" threshold is not universal. It is use-case specific, and it depends on three factors: the cost of being wrong, the cost of not having the feature at all, and the availability of a human correction path. When wrong is cheap and correctable, good enough can be 80 percent. When wrong is expensive or irreversible, good enough might need to be 99 percent, and anything below that should route to human review.

I worked with a team that spent four months trying to get their document classification system from 91 percent accuracy to 95 percent accuracy. They tried better prompts, more context, chain-of-thought reasoning, ensemble approaches. They got to 93 percent and stalled. During those four months, the 91 percent version sat unused in staging while the operations team continued classifying documents manually. When someone finally did the math, the 91 percent version would have saved the operations team roughly 300 hours of manual work over those four months, even accounting for the time needed to correct the 9 percent of errors. The pursuit of the last 4 percent of accuracy cost more than the errors it was trying to eliminate.

This is not an argument against quality. It is an argument for economic clarity about where to invest your engineering time. Sometimes the right move is to ship at 91 percent with a good correction workflow and invest those four months in a different feature that delivers more total value. Sometimes the domain demands 99 percent and you have to do the hard work to get there. The failure mode is not choosing wrong. It is not choosing at all, defaulting to a vague sense that the system should be "better" without quantifying what better means or what it costs.

The discipline here is in setting the threshold deliberately rather than discovering it through user complaints. Define what good enough means for each feature before you ship it. Write it down. Measure against it. Adjust it as you learn more. This is not lowering your standards. It is calibrating them to the reality of how probabilistic systems behave, which is exactly what an engineer is supposed to do: design for the system you actually have, not the one you wish you had.

Failure Modes and Tolerances

Every system fails. What distinguishes well-engineered systems from poorly-engineered ones is not the absence of failure but the presence of a clear understanding of how the system fails and what happens when it does.

In deterministic software, failure is usually binary and visible. The system throws an error, returns the wrong result, or crashes. You get a stack trace. You can reproduce the bug. You fix it, write a regression test, and move on. The failure mode is specific, identifiable, and eliminable.

In probabilistic software, failure is often partial and invisible. The system does not crash. It does not throw an error. It returns an output that looks plausible but is subtly wrong, or slightly less good than it used to be, or correct for most users but misleading for a specific subset. There is no stack trace. The failure is distributed across a population of outputs, and no single output is clearly broken. This makes probabilistic failures harder to detect, harder to diagnose, and harder to fix. It also means your monitoring strategy needs to be fundamentally different from what you use for deterministic systems.

AI systems have failure modes that traditional software does not. It is worth naming them explicitly, because you cannot design around failures you have not categorized.

Hallucination. The model generates information that sounds plausible but is factually incorrect. This is probably the most discussed failure mode, but it is not always the most dangerous. Hallucinated facts in a casual chatbot are awkward. Hallucinated facts in a medical or legal system are liabilities. The severity depends on context, but the failure mode exists in every system that generates text, and you need a plan for it.

Drift. Model behavior changes over time, either because the provider updates the model or because your input distribution shifts. A prompt that worked well three months ago might produce subtly different results today, not because you changed anything, but because the model underneath changed. Drift is insidious because it is gradual. You do not get an error message. You get a slow degradation in output quality that is hard to notice without systematic measurement.

Boundary confusion. The model handles inputs that fall near the boundary of what it was designed for in unpredictable ways. Ask it to classify a clearly positive review as positive, and it will. Ask it to classify a mildly sarcastic review that is ambiguously positive, and you will get inconsistent results. Every classification, extraction, or decision task has boundary inputs, and the model's behavior on those boundaries is where most production issues originate.

Format violation. You asked for JSON. You got mostly JSON, with a conversational preamble the model decided to include. You asked for a three-sentence summary. You got five sentences. Format violations are the most mechanically straightforward failure to handle, and yet an alarming number of production systems have no validation between the model's output and the next step in the pipeline. The fix is simple: validate output structure before acting on it, and have a retry or fallback path when validation fails.

Refusal and over-caution. The model declines to perform a legitimate task because it interprets the request as potentially harmful or outside its guidelines. This is more common than most teams expect, and it tends to appear on the exact inputs that are most valuable to your users: the complex, ambiguous, edge-case inputs that are the reason they are using your tool in the first place. Designing around refusals means having fallback strategies and, in some cases, restructuring your prompts to avoid triggering unnecessary caution.

For each of these failure modes, the engineering question is not "how do I prevent this?" You cannot fully prevent any of them. The question is "what is my tolerance for this failure, and what does my system do when it occurs?"

Tolerance is specific and measurable. You might say: "We accept that hallucination will occur in approximately 3 percent of outputs. For those cases, the user sees a confidence indicator and a link to source materials so they can verify independently. If hallucination rates exceed 5 percent on any weekly cohort, an alert fires and we investigate." That is an engineering specification. It treats the failure mode as a known property of the system rather than an anomaly to be eliminated. It defines what acceptable looks like, what the user experience should be when failure occurs, and what triggers an escalation.

Compare that to the more common approach: "We hope the model does not hallucinate, and if users report problems we will look into it." That is not engineering. That is wishful thinking dressed up in a support process.

The discipline of defining failure tolerances upfront changes how you build. It forces you to think about monitoring before you ship. It forces you to build confidence scoring into your pipeline. It forces you to design user experiences that are honest about uncertainty instead of pretending the system is always right. All of these are improvements to the system regardless of whether the specific failure they were designed for ever occurs. Systems built with explicit failure tolerances are better systems, period, because the act of planning for failure makes every other part of the design more robust.

There is also an organizational dimension worth noting. When a team has explicit failure tolerances, conversations about quality become productive instead of adversarial. Instead of arguing about whether the system is "good enough" in the abstract, the team can look at the data: are we within our defined tolerances or not? If you are within tolerance, ship and move on. If you are outside tolerance, the data tells you exactly which failure mode to address and by how much. This removes the ambiguity that leads to either premature shipping or endless polishing, both of which are expensive in different ways. Clear tolerances turn subjective quality debates into engineering problems, and engineering problems are what your team is best equipped to solve.

Engineering Heuristics

These heuristics operationalize the shift from deterministic to probabilistic thinking. They are meant to be applied during design, during code review, and during retrospectives when something goes wrong.

Heuristic 1: Design for the 90th percentile, not the happy path.

The happy path in an AI system is the input that is clear, unambiguous, and well within the model's capabilities. Your system will handle that input beautifully without much effort from you. The 90th percentile is the input that is slightly messy, slightly ambiguous, or slightly outside the expected range. That is where your design effort should go, because that is where your users will discover whether your system is trustworthy or fragile. When you review a feature design, do not ask "does this work for the typical case?" Ask "what happens for the hardest 10 percent of inputs that are still within scope?" The answer to that question will tell you more about the quality of your design than any demo scenario.

Heuristic 2: Never hardcode expected outputs in AI tests.

This is the most common testing mistake teams make when they start building with AI. They write a test that sends a prompt and asserts that the response equals a specific string. The test passes today and fails tomorrow when the model updates, even though the output quality has not changed at all. The response was slightly rephrased, or the order of information shifted, or the model added a clause it did not include before. The test is not measuring quality. It is measuring exact reproduction, and exact reproduction is not a property of probabilistic systems. Instead, test for properties: does the output contain the required information? Does it conform to the expected schema? Does it stay within the specified length? Does it avoid known failure patterns? Property-based tests survive model updates because they test what matters rather than what happened to be true yesterday.

Heuristic 3: Define acceptable variance before you build, not after.

Before you write the first line of code for an AI feature, answer these questions: What does a good output look like? What does an acceptable but imperfect output look like? What does an unacceptable output look like? What is the expected ratio between these categories? What happens in the user experience for each category? If you cannot answer these questions, you are not ready to build the feature. You will end up building it, shipping it, discovering the answers through user complaints, and then retrofitting the handling you should have designed from the start. Defining variance upfront is faster, cheaper, and produces a better outcome than discovering it in production.

Probabilistic thinking is not a compromise. It is not a concession to the imperfection of current models that will be resolved when models get better. It is the correct way to reason about a category of systems that are, by their nature, not deterministic. Models will get better. They will still be probabilistic. The outputs will be more reliably good, but they will not be identical across runs. The variance will narrow, but it will not disappear. Designing for that reality is not a temporary workaround. It is sound engineering for the systems you are actually building, today and for the foreseeable future.

The practical payoff of embracing probabilistic thinking shows up everywhere in the chapters that follow. When we discuss context architecture in Part II, the reason context management matters so much is that it shifts the probability distribution of outputs toward the acceptable end. Better context means a narrower, more favorable distribution. When we discuss evaluation in Part V, the reason eval-first development is essential is that you cannot manage a distribution you are not measuring. When we discuss graceful degradation in Chapter 10, the reason fallback paths are first-class architectural components is that a probabilistic system has a nonzero failure rate by definition, and pretending otherwise is not an option.

In Chapter 1, we established that the model is infrastructure, not product. In this chapter, we established that the infrastructure is probabilistic, not deterministic. Together, these two principles form the foundation for everything that follows. You are building a product layer on top of a probabilistic infrastructure. The next question is: what do you feed that infrastructure to get the best possible results? That is the subject of Part II, starting with context as architecture.

Context is Architecture

Part II: Context

---

*Context windows are not just input fields.
They are the primary architectural surface
in AI-driven applications. How you
structure, curate, and inject context
determines the quality of every response
your system produces.*

The Context Window as Architecture

Most engineers encounter the context window for the
first time as a text box. You type something in, the
model responds. It feels like a chat field. It feels like a
search bar. It feels like an input field on a form. That
initial impression is misleading, and it creates a
mental model that actively holds teams back from
building good AI systems.

The context window is not an input field. It is the
primary architectural surface of your entire
application. Every piece of information the model
uses to generate a response, every instruction, every
constraint, every example, every retrieved document,

every piece of conversation history, lives in that window. The model sees nothing else. It has no memory outside the window. It has no access to information not placed there. The quality of the output is bounded by the quality of what you put into that space.

Think about what that means in practice. If you are building a customer support system and the model gives a wrong answer about a product feature, the cause is almost never that the model is incapable of answering correctly. The cause is almost always that the right information was not in the context window when the model needed it. Either the retrieval system did not surface the relevant documentation, or the documentation was there but buried under irrelevant content, or the information was structured in a way the model could not use effectively. The architecture of the context window, what goes in, how it is structured, in what order, is the architecture of your system's intelligence.

This is a stronger claim than it might first appear. In traditional software, the primary architectural surface is your data model, your API layer, your service boundaries. The code is the system. In AI-driven software, the code matters, but the context window is where the actual reasoning happens. Two systems with identical code but different context strategies will produce dramatically different output quality. The context window is the bottleneck, and bottlenecks are where architectural attention pays the highest dividends.

When I say "context is architecture," I mean it should receive the same engineering rigor you give to any other core architectural decision. You should design your context structures deliberately. You should document them. You should version them. You should test them. You should monitor their impact on output quality. And you should treat changes to your context strategy with the same care you would treat changes to your database schema, because the downstream effects are equally consequential.

The teams that build the best AI systems are, almost without exception, the teams that take context engineering the most seriously. Not prompt engineering. Not model selection. Context engineering. The gap between a mediocre AI product and an excellent one is usually a gap in how well the context pipeline works, and that gap is entirely within the engineering team's control.

I want to illustrate this with a debugging scenario that I have seen repeat across multiple teams. A system that generates product descriptions for an e-commerce platform starts producing descriptions that include incorrect specifications. The team's first instinct is to adjust the prompt: add stronger instructions about accuracy, include more examples of correct descriptions, add a warning about not making up specifications. These changes help marginally, but the core problem persists.

When someone finally inspects the actual context window for the failing cases, the problem is immediately visible. The retrieval system is pulling product data from an internal database, but the data includes fields from related products that share the same category tag. The model is seeing specifications for three different products and doing its best to synthesize a description from all of them. The fix is not a prompt change. It is a context change: filter the retrieved data to include only the specific product, not the category.

This pattern, model blamed for a context problem, is so common that it should be the default hypothesis when something goes wrong. The model is usually doing a reasonable job with the information it has. The question is whether the information it has is the information it needs. That is a context architecture question, and it is the question this entire chapter is built around.

Context Injection Patterns

Context does not magically appear in the window. It is assembled, and the way you assemble it is a design decision with real consequences. There are several common patterns for injecting context, and understanding when to use each one is a core competency of AI engineering.

Static context is information that does not change between requests. Your system prompt is static context. So are the behavioral instructions, output format specifications, and role definitions you include in every call. Static context is the foundation of the window, the part that establishes what the system is and how it should behave. The design challenge with static context is keeping it focused. It is tempting to pack your system prompt with every instruction, caveat, and edge case you can think of. The result is a bloated prompt that dilutes the model's attention across too many directives. Effective static context is precise: it includes exactly what the model needs for every request and nothing more.

Dynamic context is information that changes per request based on the specific input or situation. If a user asks a question about their account, the dynamic context includes their account data, their recent activity, and any relevant settings. Dynamic context is where most of the engineering complexity lives, because you need to decide, for each request, what information is relevant, how much of it to include, and how to structure it so the model can use it effectively. Too much dynamic context and you drown the model in noise. Too little and the model lacks the information it needs. Getting this balance right is the subject of Chapter 4, but the architectural point here is that your dynamic context pipeline, the code that selects, retrieves, and formats context for each request, is a critical system component that deserves its own testing, monitoring, and iteration cycle.

Retrieved context is a specific form of dynamic context where information is pulled from an external store, typically a vector database or search index, based on the user's query. This is the core of retrieval-augmented generation, which we will discuss in more detail in the next section. The design challenge with retrieved context is relevance: the retrieval system needs to find the right information and rank it appropriately. A retrieval system that returns the top five documents by semantic similarity is not necessarily returning the five most useful documents. Relevance is task-dependent, and your retrieval strategy should be tuned for the specific kinds of questions your system handles.

Conversation history is context from previous turns in a multi-turn interaction. This is straightforward in concept but tricky in practice, because conversation history grows with every turn, and context windows have finite capacity. Naive approaches include the full history until it runs out of space. Better approaches summarize older turns, preserving key information while reducing token consumption. The best approaches selectively include history based on relevance to the current turn, treating conversation history as a retrieval problem rather than a concatenation problem.

These patterns are not mutually exclusive. A well-designed context window typically combines all four: a focused system prompt (static), relevant user or session data (dynamic), retrieved documents or knowledge (retrieved), and selected conversation history. The architecture is in how you compose these layers, how you prioritize between them when space is limited, and how you structure each piece so the model can distinguish between instructions, reference material, and conversational context.

A useful mental model: think of the context window as a briefing document you are preparing for a very capable but uninformed colleague. They know nothing about this specific task other than what you put in the document. The quality of their work depends entirely on the quality of the briefing. You would not hand them a disorganized pile of every document in your filing cabinet. You would select the relevant materials, organize them clearly, and provide instructions about what you need and in what format. That is exactly what good context engineering does for the model.

The order of context layers matters more than most teams realize. Models, like humans reading a long document, pay more attention to what appears at the beginning and at the end of the window. Content in the middle gets less attention, particularly in long contexts. This has practical implications for how you compose your layers. System instructions should appear first, establishing the behavioral framework. The user's current query should appear near the end, keeping it fresh in the model's attention. Retrieved documents and conversation history occupy the middle, organized by relevance so the most important information is closest to the query. There is no single correct ordering, and it varies by use case, but the ordering should be a deliberate design decision, not an accident of how the code concatenates strings.

A common architectural mistake is to assemble context in a single function call with no separation between layers. This makes it difficult to debug, test, or modify any individual layer without affecting the others. A better approach is to build your context as a pipeline of distinct stages: one stage that prepares the system prompt, another that retrieves relevant documents, another that selects and formats conversation history, another that assembles the user's query with any necessary framing. Each stage can be tested independently, monitored separately, and modified without disrupting the others. This is separation of concerns applied to the context window, and it pays the same dividends here that it pays everywhere else in software engineering.

Retrieval-Augmented Generation

Retrieval-augmented generation, or RAG, has become the default architecture for AI systems that need to work with knowledge beyond what the model was trained on. The concept is straightforward: instead of relying solely on the model's internal knowledge, you retrieve relevant documents from an external source and include them in the context window alongside the user's query. The model then generates its response using both its trained knowledge and the retrieved information.

The concept is simple. The engineering is not.

A RAG pipeline has several components, and each one is a potential point of failure. You need a document store that holds your knowledge base. You need an ingestion pipeline that processes raw documents into chunks suitable for retrieval. You need an embedding model that converts those chunks into vector representations. You need a vector database or search index that stores and queries those embeddings. You need a retrieval strategy that selects which chunks to include in the context. And you need a composition step that assembles the retrieved chunks alongside the system prompt, user query, and any other context into a coherent window.

Each of these components involves design decisions that significantly affect output quality. The chunking strategy alone can make or break a RAG system. Chunk too large and you waste context space on irrelevant information that dilutes the model's focus. Chunk too small and you lose the coherence needed to answer questions that span multiple paragraphs or require understanding of document structure. Chunk on arbitrary token boundaries and you split sentences, tables, and logical sections in ways that make the content unusable or misleading.

The right chunking strategy depends on the structure of your documents, the kinds of questions your users ask, and the context window budget you are working with. Legal documents should be chunked on clause boundaries. Technical documentation should be chunked on section boundaries. Meeting notes might be chunked by topic or by speaker. The universal truth is that document-aware chunking, chunking that respects the natural structure of the content, outperforms naive fixed-size chunking in almost every case. It is more work to implement, because you need to understand the structure of your documents. But it is the kind of work that pays off on every single query.

Retrieval ranking is equally consequential. Semantic similarity, the default ranking in most vector databases, measures how close the query embedding is to the chunk embedding. But semantic similarity does not always correspond to usefulness. A chunk might be semantically similar to the query because it uses the same vocabulary, even though it answers a different question entirely. A chunk that uses different vocabulary might contain exactly the information needed but rank lower because the surface-level language is different. Effective retrieval often requires a reranking step that goes beyond raw similarity to assess actual relevance to the specific question being asked. This can be done with a secondary model, with keyword matching as a supplement to semantic search, or with domain-specific scoring logic that weights certain document types or recency more heavily.

There is a common failure pattern with RAG that is worth naming explicitly: the retrieval quality death spiral. A team builds a RAG system, tests it on a handful of examples, and it works well. They ship it. Over time, the document store grows. New documents are added without being reviewed for quality or consistency. Some documents are outdated but not removed. Some cover the same topic with conflicting information. The retrieval system starts surfacing lower-quality or contradictory chunks, and the model's output quality degrades. The team blames the model and starts prompt engineering workarounds, when the real problem is upstream in the retrieval pipeline. By the time they realize this, the document store is a mess and cleaning it up is a significant project.

The antidote is to treat your document store and your retrieval pipeline with the same discipline you apply to a production database. Content quality matters. Indexing strategy matters. Stale content needs to be identified and removed or updated. Retrieval quality should be measured independently of generation quality. If you cannot tell whether the retrieval step returned the right documents, you cannot diagnose whether a bad output was caused by the model or by the context.

A useful practice: build a retrieval evaluation suite that is separate from your generation evaluation suite. For a set of representative queries, document what the ideal retrieved chunks should be. Run those queries regularly and measure retrieval precision and recall independently. This gives you an early warning system for retrieval degradation. If retrieval quality drops, you know the problem is in your document store or your indexing, not in the model. If retrieval quality holds steady but generation quality drops, you know to look at the prompt or the model. This separation of concerns in evaluation mirrors the separation of concerns in the architecture itself, and it is one of the most valuable diagnostic capabilities you can build.

This is a point I will return to in Chapter 4 on signal over noise: the retrieval system is not just a pipe. It is a filter. Its job is not to find anything that looks relevant. Its job is to find the specific information the model needs to answer this specific question well, and to exclude everything else. The better your filter, the better your model's output. There is no amount of prompt engineering that can compensate for consistently bad retrieval.

Managing Context at Scale

Context management gets more complex as your system grows, along several dimensions that are worth anticipating early.

User scale. A system serving a hundred users can afford expensive, high-quality retrieval strategies. A system serving a million users needs retrieval that is fast, efficient, and cost-effective. The optimal context strategy at scale may be different from the one that works best in testing. Caching strategies become important. Precomputing context for common query patterns can reduce latency and cost. Tiering your retrieval, using a fast but approximate first pass followed by a slower but precise reranking, can give you both speed and quality.

Knowledge scale. As your document store grows from thousands to millions of chunks, retrieval quality tends to degrade unless you invest in maintaining it. More documents mean more potential false positives in retrieval. Category boundaries blur. Contradictory information surfaces more frequently. You need strategies for keeping the knowledge base curated: automated quality checks, freshness scoring, duplicate detection, and periodic audits. Treating the knowledge base as a static asset that only grows is a recipe for gradual quality erosion.

Feature scale. As your application adds more AI-powered features, each with its own context requirements, you need to decide whether each feature manages its own context pipeline independently or shares a common infrastructure. The shared approach reduces duplication and makes cross-feature improvements easier, but it requires careful abstraction to avoid one feature's context needs interfering with another's. The independent approach is simpler initially but leads to divergent context strategies that are hard to unify later. Most teams that grow past three or four AI features eventually need a shared context platform with feature-specific configuration.

Conversation scale. Multi-turn conversations accumulate context with every turn. In a system that handles long conversations, such as a technical support agent that works through complex issues over many exchanges, the conversation history can easily exceed the context window. You need a strategy for compression: summarizing older turns, selectively including only the turns relevant to the current question, or maintaining a running summary that gets updated rather than appended. The choice depends on how much historical detail matters for later turns. A customer support conversation might need to remember specific details from turn three to resolve an issue at turn fifteen. A creative brainstorming session might only need the most recent direction.

The common thread across all of these scaling dimensions is that context management is not a one-time design decision. It is an ongoing operational discipline. The context strategy that works at launch is not the one you will need six months later. Building with that in mind, making your context pipeline configurable, measurable, and iteratable, is the difference between a system that scales gracefully and one that hits a quality wall as it grows.

There is also a cost dimension to context at scale that deserves explicit attention. Every token in the context window has a direct monetary cost in API pricing. A system that includes 4,000 tokens of context per request costs four times as much as one that achieves the same output quality with 1,000 tokens. When you are processing a hundred requests a day, the difference is negligible. When you are processing a million requests a day, the difference is significant enough to affect product economics. Context optimization is cost optimization, and at scale, the engineering investment in reducing context size while maintaining quality pays for itself quickly.

This creates a healthy engineering tension: you want to include enough context for the model to produce high-quality output, but you want to minimize the context size for cost and latency reasons. The resolution is not to pick a side but to measure the trade-off explicitly. Run experiments: what happens to output quality when you reduce retrieved context from five chunks to three? From three to two? At what point does quality degrade below your acceptable threshold? The answers will tell you exactly how much context you can afford to remove and how much you need to keep. This is empirical work, not guesswork, and it should be part of your regular optimization cycle.

System Prompts as Contracts

The system prompt is the single most important piece of static context in your application. It defines who the model is, what it does, how it behaves, what it refuses to do, and what format its output should take. For many applications, the system prompt is the primary differentiator between a raw model API and a useful product. And despite this importance, system prompts are, in most teams I have observed, the least rigorously managed artifact in the entire codebase.

System prompts tend to evolve through accretion. Someone writes an initial prompt. Someone else adds a clause to handle an edge case. A third person adds behavioral instructions to address a user complaint. Over weeks and months, the prompt grows into a long, unstructured document full of contradictory instructions, redundant clauses, and implicit assumptions that nobody remembers making. It lives in a string constant somewhere in the codebase, or worse, in an environment variable or a configuration file with no version history. Changes to it are not reviewed with the same rigor as code changes, despite the fact that a system prompt change can affect every single response the application produces.

This is the wrong way to manage the most consequential artifact in your system. The right way is to treat the system prompt as a contract.

A contract has specific properties that system prompts should share. It is versioned: you can see exactly what changed between version 4 and version 5, and you can roll back if a change causes problems. It is reviewed: changes go through a review process where someone other than the author evaluates whether the change is correct and whether it might have unintended side effects. It is tested: you have a suite of evaluation cases that verify the system behaves correctly under the contract, and you run them before deploying any change. It is documented: there is an explanation of why each section of the prompt exists and what behavior it is intended to produce.

In practice, this means your system prompt should live in version control, in a dedicated file or set of files, not embedded in application code. Changes to the system prompt should require a pull request and a review, just like code changes. You should have an evaluation suite that runs automatically when the system prompt changes, checking that the modification did not degrade behavior on known test cases. And the prompt itself should include comments or an accompanying document that explains the purpose of each section.

The contract metaphor extends to how you think about the relationship between the system prompt and the rest of your context pipeline. The system prompt defines the model's role and behavior. The dynamic context provides the information specific to each request. The boundary between these two should be clear and intentional. Instructions that apply to every request belong in the system prompt.

Information that varies per request belongs in the dynamic context. When this boundary blurs, when request-specific instructions creep into the system prompt or universal behavior rules get stuffed into per-request context, the system becomes harder to reason about and harder to test.

There is a structural benefit to the contract approach that goes beyond code hygiene. When your system prompt is well-documented and versioned, you can reason about the impact of changes before you make them. If you want to add a new behavioral rule, you can evaluate it against your existing test suite and see whether it conflicts with existing rules. If you want to change the output format, you can trace all the downstream code that parses that format and update it in the same change. This is basic software engineering practice applied to an artifact that is often treated as a casual, informal string. The system prompt deserves better, because it does more.

Let me illustrate the difference between a prompt managed casually and one managed as a contract. A casually managed prompt might look like this: a single string that says something like, "You are a helpful customer support agent. Be friendly and concise. Always check the knowledge base before answering. If you do not know the answer, say so. Format responses in markdown. Do not make up information. The user's name is included in the message. Use it when greeting them." This prompt works for simple cases, but it contains ambiguities that will surface as bugs. What does "concise" mean? Two sentences? Two paragraphs? What happens when the knowledge base returns conflicting information? What does "say so" look like in practice?

A contract-managed prompt addresses these questions explicitly. Each section is labeled with its purpose. Behavioral instructions are separated from formatting rules. Ambiguous terms are defined: "concise" means two to four sentences unless the question requires a longer explanation. Fallback behavior is specified: if the knowledge base returns no relevant results, respond with a specific template that acknowledges the limitation and offers to escalate to a human agent. Edge cases are documented: if conflicting information is found, surface both sources with a note about the discrepancy rather than choosing one silently. Each of these specifics can be tested independently, reviewed by stakeholders, and updated without risk of unintended side effects.

The effort to manage system prompts as contracts is modest compared to the value it delivers. You are spending the time one way or another, either upfront in careful design and documentation, or later in debugging mysterious quality issues, reconciling contradictory instructions, and explaining to users why the system behaved differently this week than it did last week. The upfront investment is always cheaper.

Engineering Heuristics

Heuristic 1: Treat your system prompt like an API contract.

Your system prompt defines the behavior that every user interaction depends on. It deserves version control, code review, automated testing, and documentation. A change to your system prompt is at least as consequential as a change to a public API endpoint. If you would not deploy an API change without review, testing, and a rollback plan, do not deploy a system prompt change without them either. This is not overhead. It is the minimum standard for managing an artifact that affects 100 percent of your output. As a practical starting point: move your system prompt into a dedicated file in version control today. Add a comment explaining the purpose of each section. Set up a simple eval that runs five to ten representative queries against any change. You can do this in an afternoon, and it will prevent the next system prompt edit from causing a production surprise.

Heuristic 2: Version your context structures the same way you version code.

Your context pipeline, the logic that selects, retrieves, formats, and assembles context for each request, should be versioned, tested, and deployed with the same discipline as application code. When output quality changes, you need to be able to answer the question: did we change the context? Version control on your context structures gives you that ability. It also lets you A/B test context strategies, roll back changes that degrade quality, and track the relationship between context changes and output metrics over time. Teams that manage context informally lose the ability to diagnose quality issues, because they cannot distinguish between a model problem and a context problem. The first time you have to debug a quality regression without knowing whether the context pipeline changed, you will wish you had versioned it from the start.

Heuristic 3: If the model is confused, look at the context first.

When the model produces a bad output, the instinct is to blame the model or reach for a prompt fix. Before you do either, inspect the actual context window for that specific request. What did the model actually see? Was the relevant information present? Was it buried under irrelevant information? Was it structured in a way the model could parse? Were there contradictory instructions or conflicting source documents? In my experience, at least 70 percent of output quality issues trace back to a context problem, not a model problem or a prompt problem. Build tooling that lets you inspect the full context window for any request in your system, including in production. This capability is one of the highest-value debugging investments you can make. The context window is the first place to look and the last place most teams check. Reverse that habit.

Context is the architectural surface where your engineering has the most leverage over output quality. The model is capable. What it produces depends on what you give it to work with. If you give it a well-structured briefing with relevant information, clear instructions, and appropriate constraints, it will produce good work. If you give it a disorganized dump of loosely related content, it will do its best, but its best will be noticeably worse. The difference between these two outcomes is not the model. It is the engineering work you did or did not do before the model ever saw the input.

This chapter established context management as a first-class engineering discipline: something that deserves the same rigor, tooling, and organizational attention as your data layer, your API design, or your deployment pipeline. The next chapter narrows the focus to a specific and critical aspect of that discipline: the difference between signal and noise, and why filling a large context window is not the same thing as filling it well.

Signal Over Noise

Part II: Context

More context is not always better context. Stuffing a model with irrelevant information degrades output quality. The discipline of signal extraction is one of the most underrated skills in AI engineering.

Relevance and Retrieval Quality

Chapter 3 established that the context window is the primary architectural surface of your AI system. This chapter is about what goes into that surface and, just as importantly, what should be kept out.

The natural instinct when building an AI system is to give the model as much information as possible. Bigger context windows should be better, right? More knowledge means better answers. If you have a 200,000-token window, why not fill it? The reasoning feels sound. It is also wrong.

More context is only better when all of the context is relevant. When irrelevant information enters the context window, it does not sit inertly waiting to be ignored. It actively competes for the model's attention. It introduces ambiguity. It creates paths for the model to wander down instead of staying focused on the actual question. A model that has to sift through ten pages of barely-related documentation to find the two paragraphs that answer the user's question will produce a worse response than one that sees only those two paragraphs. Not always worse. Not dramatically worse on average inputs. But measurably, consistently worse on the kinds of nuanced, specific, or ambiguous inputs where quality matters most.

This is the signal-to-noise problem, and it exists at every layer of your context pipeline. It exists in your retrieval system, which might return five documents when only two are relevant. It exists in your chunking strategy, which might include the surrounding paragraphs of a relevant section even though those paragraphs add nothing. It exists in your conversation history, which might include twenty turns when only the last three are relevant to the current question. It exists in your system prompt, which might include instructions for edge cases that apply to one percent of requests but dilute the model's attention on the other ninety-nine percent.

The discipline of signal over noise is the discipline of ruthless curation. For every piece of information that enters the context window, you should be able to answer the question: how does this help the model produce a better response to this specific query? If the answer is "it might help" or "it could not hurt," that is not good enough. In a context window, everything that is not signal is noise, and noise has a cost even when it does not look harmful.

Relevance is the operational word, and it is more nuanced than it appears. A document about the same topic as the user's query is not necessarily relevant to the user's query. A user asking "what is the refund policy for enterprise customers?" needs the enterprise refund policy, not the general refund policy, not the returns policy, not the terms of service page that mentions refunds in passing, and not the blog post about how the company redesigned its refund process last year. All of those are topically related. Only one actually answers the question. Your retrieval system needs to distinguish between topical similarity and genuine relevance, and that distinction is where most of the engineering work lives.

I will offer a concrete example that illustrates how relevance failures compound. A team building an internal knowledge assistant for a large company had a vector database with around 40,000 chunks indexed from internal documentation: engineering runbooks, product specs, onboarding guides, meeting notes, policy documents, and archived Slack threads that someone decided to index for completeness. When a new engineer asked the system "how do I request access to the production database?" the retrieval system returned five chunks. Two were from the current access request runbook. One was from a three-year-old onboarding guide that described a different, now-deprecated process. One was a meeting note where someone discussed changing the access process. One was from a document about a different database entirely that happened to mention production access in passing.

The model, doing its best with what it had, synthesized an answer that blended the current process with the deprecated one and included an irrelevant detail from the wrong database's documentation. The answer was plausible, mostly correct, and subtly wrong in a way that cost the new engineer two hours of following the wrong steps. The model was not at fault. The retrieval system returned context with a roughly 40 percent noise ratio, and the model processed all of it faithfully. The fix was not a better prompt. It was better retrieval: removing the archived content from the index, filtering out meeting notes for factual queries, and adding a recency bias so current documentation ranked above historical content.

This kind of failure is extremely common and extremely underdiagnosed. The output looks reasonable. The user might not even realize it was wrong until they act on it. And the root cause is invisible unless you specifically inspect the context window to see what the model was working with. Signal over noise is not just about making outputs better on average. It is about eliminating the class of failures where the model gives a confidently wrong answer because the context led it there.

Token Economics

Every token in the context window has a cost. That cost is both financial and cognitive, and understanding both dimensions is important for making good engineering decisions.

The financial cost is straightforward. Model providers charge per token, and context tokens are a major component of the bill. A system that includes 8,000 tokens of context per request costs roughly twice as much as one that achieves the same output quality with 4,000 tokens. At small scale, this difference is a rounding error. At the scale of a production system handling hundreds of thousands of requests per day, it is a line item significant enough to affect product margins. Teams that ignore token economics during development discover them when the invoice arrives.

The cognitive cost is less obvious but often more important. The model has a finite attention budget. While modern models can technically process very long contexts, their ability to use information effectively is not uniform across the entire window. Research has consistently shown that models attend more strongly to information at the beginning and end of the context and less strongly to information in the middle, particularly in very long contexts. This means that stuffing the window with more content does not just cost more money. It can actively degrade the model's ability to use the information that matters.

Think about it from the model's perspective. If you give it a 2,000-token context where every token is relevant, it can focus entirely on useful information. If you give it a 20,000-token context where 2,000 tokens are relevant and 18,000 are noise, it has to identify the signal within a ten-to-one noise ratio. It will still find the relevant information most of the time, but its accuracy on complex or nuanced questions will be lower, its reasoning will be less focused, and its outputs will be more likely to incorporate irrelevant details from the noise.

Token economics creates a healthy optimization pressure: every token should earn its place. This does not mean you should minimize context at all costs. It means you should be intentional about what you include and have a reason for every piece of content that enters the window. If you cannot explain why a particular chunk is in the context, it probably should not be there. And if you can explain why but the reason is "just in case," that is a signal to measure whether it actually helps before committing to including it on every request.

There is a latency dimension to token economics as well. More tokens in the context mean longer processing time, which means higher latency for the user. In interactive applications where users are waiting for a response, the difference between a 3,000-token context and a 15,000-token context can be the difference between a response that feels snappy and one that feels sluggish. Users are surprisingly sensitive to response latency in AI products, partly because they are often comparing the experience to asking a question of a human colleague who responds in seconds. Every unnecessary token in the context slows the response down and degrades the user experience, independent of any effect on output quality.

The practical discipline here is to set a context budget for each feature and optimize within it. Not a hard limit that the system crashes against, but a target that the team works toward. Something like: "For this feature, our target context size is 3,000 tokens of retrieved content plus 500 tokens of system prompt plus the user's query. If we need to exceed that budget, we need to justify it with evidence that the additional context improves output quality." This kind of discipline prevents the common drift pattern where context size grows gradually over time as engineers add "one more thing" without removing anything, until the window is bloated and the team has lost track of what is actually contributing to output quality.

Noise as a Failure Mode

In traditional software, noise is an annoyance. A log file full of irrelevant entries makes debugging harder but does not change the behavior of the system. In AI systems, noise is a failure mode. It actively degrades output quality, and it does so in ways that are subtle enough to miss unless you are specifically looking for them.

There are several distinct ways that noise causes failures in practice.

Diluted attention. When relevant information is surrounded by irrelevant content, the model's ability to focus on what matters decreases. The effect is most pronounced on questions that require precise extraction or careful reasoning. A model that needs to find a specific contractual term buried in a context window full of tangentially related clauses will occasionally extract the wrong term or conflate it with similar language from a different clause. The same model given only the relevant clause would not make that mistake. The noise did not just fail to help. It actively caused an error.

Contradictory context. When your context includes multiple sources that address the same topic but with different or outdated information, the model has to decide which source to trust. It does not always decide correctly. If your retrieval system surfaces a current policy document and an old blog post that describes a previous version of the policy, the model might blend the two, producing a response that is neither the current policy nor the old one. The fix is not better prompting. It is better curation: removing the outdated content from the retrieval pool entirely.

Instruction dilution. Every instruction in the system prompt competes for the model's attention. A system prompt with five clear, focused instructions will produce more consistent behavior than one with thirty instructions covering every conceivable edge case. This is counterintuitive for engineers who are used to being thorough. But in a probabilistic system, the relationship between instruction count and behavioral compliance is not linear. At some point, adding more instructions starts reducing compliance with the instructions that were already there. The model has a finite capacity for tracking and applying constraints simultaneously, and exceeding that capacity means that some constraints will be intermittently ignored.

Distracted reasoning. On complex tasks that require multi-step reasoning, irrelevant context can derail the reasoning chain. If the model is working through a comparison of two options and the context includes detailed information about a third option that is not being compared, the model may incorporate that third option into its analysis unprompted. The context made a tangential connection available, and the model followed it. In a focused context, that tangent would not exist, and the reasoning would stay on track.

The common thread is that noise is not neutral. In a deterministic system, extra data that is not needed is simply ignored by the code. In a probabilistic system, extra data is not ignored by the model. It is processed, weighted, and potentially incorporated into the output. This is a fundamental difference in how these systems behave, and it means that context curation is not a nice-to-have optimization. It is a reliability requirement.

If you are coming from traditional software engineering, the closest analogy is probably SQL injection, not in the security sense, but in the structural sense. In SQL injection, unvalidated user input changes the behavior of the system in unintended ways. In noisy context, unvalidated retrieval results change the behavior of the model in unintended ways. The mechanism is different, but the principle is the same: inputs that you do not control and do not validate will eventually cause behavior you did not intend. The response in both cases is the same: validate, filter, and curate what enters the system before it reaches the component that acts on it.

Chunking and Ranking Strategies

If noise is a failure mode, then the chunking and ranking strategies in your retrieval pipeline are your primary defense against it. These two components determine what information the model sees, and getting them right is one of the highest-leverage investments in your entire system.

Chunking is about how you break source documents into pieces that can be independently retrieved and assembled into context. Chapter 3 introduced the basics: document-aware chunking that respects natural structure outperforms naive fixed-size chunking. But there is more to it than choosing the right boundaries.

Chunk granularity should match query granularity. If your users typically ask specific, narrow questions, your chunks should be small enough to answer those questions without including a lot of surrounding material. If your users ask broad, conceptual questions that require synthesizing information from across a document, your chunks should be larger and structured to preserve that broader context. There is no universally correct chunk size. There is only the chunk size that matches how your users actually query your system, and you learn that by analyzing real queries, not by guessing.

Overlapping chunks reduce boundary failures. When you split a document into non-overlapping chunks, any information that spans a chunk boundary is split across two chunks, and the retrieval system might return one but not the other. Adding overlap, where each chunk includes some content from the adjacent chunks, reduces this problem. The trade-off is increased storage and slightly redundant retrieval results, but for most systems the boundary-failure reduction is worth it. An overlap of 10 to 20 percent of the chunk size is a reasonable starting point.

Metadata enrichment makes retrieval smarter. A chunk stored as raw text gives the retrieval system only one signal to work with: semantic similarity. A chunk stored with metadata, such as the source document title, the section heading, the document date, the document type, and any relevant tags, gives the retrieval system additional signals for filtering and ranking. You can filter by document type before doing semantic search. You can boost recent documents over old ones. You can require that retrieved chunks come from specific categories of source material. Metadata does not replace semantic search, but it constrains it in ways that dramatically improve precision.

Ranking determines the order in which retrieved chunks are presented to the model, and by extension, which chunks make it into the context when the window has limited space. The default ranking in most vector databases is cosine similarity between query and chunk embeddings. This is a reasonable starting point but rarely the best final answer.

A more effective approach uses a two-stage retrieval pipeline. The first stage is fast and broad: retrieve a candidate set of, say, twenty chunks using vector similarity. The second stage is slower and more precise: rerank those twenty candidates using a more sophisticated relevance model, then take the top three to five. The reranking model can consider factors that vector similarity misses: how well the chunk actually answers the question rather than just resembles it, whether the chunk contains the specific type of information the query is looking for, and whether the chunk is from a source that should be prioritized for this type of query.

The two-stage approach costs more in compute, but it produces meaningfully better context quality. And because better context quality translates directly to better output quality, the investment typically pays for itself. The first stage casts a wide net. The second stage curates. Together they implement the signal-over-noise principle at the retrieval layer.

There are a few additional ranking strategies worth considering depending on your use case. Recency weighting is valuable when your knowledge base includes documents that are updated over time. If two chunks are equally relevant by semantic similarity, but one is from a document updated last week and the other is from a document updated two years ago, the recent one should rank higher. Source authority weighting is valuable when your knowledge base includes content from sources of varying reliability. An official product specification should outrank a casual Slack message on the same topic, even if the

Slack message has higher semantic similarity to the query. These are domain-specific ranking signals, and they require you to tag your documents with metadata at ingestion time, which is additional work that pays off in every retrieval query thereafter.

One pattern I have seen work particularly well is to maintain a small set of "retrieval test cases" alongside your generation eval suite. These are queries where you know exactly which chunks should be retrieved. You run them regularly and track whether the right chunks appear in the top results. When a new batch of documents is ingested, or when the chunking strategy changes, these test cases tell you immediately whether retrieval quality held, improved, or degraded. It is a small investment that provides early warning before retrieval problems surface as output quality problems, which are much harder to diagnose.

The Art of Context Pruning

Context pruning is the practice of removing or reducing content that is already in the context window to make room for higher-value content or to improve focus. If chunking and ranking are about selecting the right information, pruning is about removing the wrong information. It is the other side of the same coin.

Pruning applies across every context layer, not just retrieved documents.

System prompt pruning. Periodically audit your system prompt and ask of each instruction: does this measurably improve behavior, or is it there because someone thought it might help? You can test this directly. Remove an instruction, run your eval suite, and see whether the scores change. If they do not, the instruction was noise and should stay removed. If they do, the instruction earns its place. I have seen teams reduce their system prompts by 40 percent through this process, with no degradation in output quality and measurable improvement in compliance with the instructions that remained, because the model could attend to fewer directives more reliably.

Retrieved context pruning. After retrieval and reranking, apply a relevance threshold. If the best retrieved chunk scores below a minimum relevance score, do not include it at all. A context window with no retrieved information and an honest "I do not have enough information to answer this question" is better than a context window stuffed with marginally relevant content that leads the model to produce a confidently wrong answer. The absence of retrieval results is itself a signal, and your system should be designed to handle it gracefully rather than forcing content into the window regardless of quality.

Conversation history pruning. In multi-turn conversations, not every previous turn is relevant to the current query. A user who has been talking about billing for five turns and then asks a product question does not need all five billing turns in the context. Selective inclusion of conversation history, based on relevance to the current turn, produces better results than blind inclusion of everything. The simplest implementation is a sliding window that keeps only the last N turns. A better implementation uses a relevance check to decide which previous turns to include based on the current query. The best implementation maintains a running summary that preserves key information while compressing older turns into a fraction of their original token count.

Dynamic content pruning. User data and session context should be filtered to include only what is relevant to the current request. If a user has a profile with fifty fields, and the current question is about their billing address, do not include their entire profile. Include the billing information. This sounds obvious in a simple case, but in complex systems with rich user data models, the default is often to include everything because it is easier than writing selection logic. That default trades engineering effort now for degraded output quality forever. The selection logic is worth writing.

The unifying principle across all of these is that context curation is an active, ongoing process, not a one-time setup. The best context pipelines are not the ones that retrieve the most information. They are the ones that are most disciplined about what they include and what they exclude. Saying no to a piece of context is as important as saying yes, and it requires the same engineering judgment.

A practical way to build the pruning habit into your team's workflow: once a month, pick five to ten random production requests and manually inspect the full context window for each one. For every piece of content in the window, ask: did this actually help the model? Could it have been removed without affecting the output? Is there information that should have been there but was not? This exercise takes less than an hour and consistently reveals opportunities to improve the signal-to-noise ratio. Teams that do this regularly have leaner, more effective context pipelines than teams that set their context strategy once and never revisit it.

> *A context window is not a storage container. It is a stage. Everything on it should be there for a reason, and anything without a role should be in the wings.*

Engineering Heuristics

Heuristic 1: Every token in context should earn its place.

This is the governing principle of the chapter. For any piece of content in the context window, you should be able to explain how it helps the model produce a better response to this specific query. If the answer is vague, speculative, or based on habit rather than evidence, remove it and measure whether output quality changes. In most systems, the first pass at context pruning reveals that 20 to 30 percent of what is in the window is not contributing meaningfully. Removing it improves focus, reduces cost, and often improves quality. Make token auditing a regular part of your development process, not a one-time exercise.

Heuristic 2: Measure retrieval quality independently from generation quality.

You need to know whether a bad output was caused by bad retrieval or bad generation. These are different problems with different solutions. Build a retrieval evaluation suite that measures, for a set of representative queries, whether the retrieval system returned the right chunks. Track retrieval precision and recall over time. When output quality drops, check retrieval quality first. If retrieval is degraded, the fix is in the document store, the chunking strategy, or the ranking logic. If retrieval is fine but output is poor, the fix is in the prompt, the output handling, or the model. Without this separation, debugging quality issues is like debugging a system where all errors say "something went wrong." You need the diagnostic specificity to act efficiently.

Heuristic 3: When output quality drops, audit your context before your prompt.

This heuristic is worth repeating from Chapter 3 because it applies with special force here. The instinct when output quality degrades is to reach for a prompt fix: add more instructions, add more examples, add stronger constraints. But if the problem is that the context contains noisy or irrelevant information, no prompt fix will fully solve it. The model is working with bad input. Inspect the actual context window for the failing cases. Look at what the retrieval system returned. Check whether the content is relevant, current, and non-contradictory. In the majority of quality issues I have diagnosed, the context was the culprit. The prompt was fine. The model was fine. The information they were working with was the problem.

Chapters 3 and 4 form a pair. Chapter 3 established that context is architecture: the primary surface where engineering effort produces quality. This chapter established that the quality of that architecture depends on discipline as much as capability. Bigger context windows are a tool, not a solution. More retrieval results are an opportunity, not a guarantee. The teams that build the best AI systems are not the ones with the most context. They are the ones with the best curated context.

Together, these two chapters make an argument that will be tested and extended throughout the rest of the book. Every principle that follows, from prompt design to agent scoping to evaluation, depends on the quality of the context pipeline. If the context is noisy, the best prompt in the world cannot fully compensate. If the retrieval system is surfacing the wrong documents, the most carefully scoped agent will still produce unreliable outputs. If the evaluation suite does not measure retrieval quality independently, you will misdiagnose problems and apply fixes to the wrong layer. Context is not one concern among many. It is the foundation that every other concern builds on.

With the foundations set in Part I and the context discipline established in Part II, we turn next to the interface between intent and output: the prompt itself. Part III begins with Chapter 5, Prompt as Interface, which repositions prompt design as a

systems engineering discipline rather than an
informal craft.

Prompt as Interface

Part III: Prompting

A prompt is not a search query. It is an interface. The best prompts encode assumptions, constrain scope, define output formats, and account for edge cases. Writing prompts well is engineering work.

Prompt Structure and Anatomy

There is a widespread misconception that prompt engineering is a soft skill. That it is about finding clever phrasings, discovering magic words, or developing an intuition for what models respond to. Some of that intuition is real, but framing prompt design as a craft trick rather than an engineering discipline has done real damage to how teams approach it.

A prompt is an interface. It sits between human intent and machine output, and it translates one into the other. In that sense, it serves the same function as an API endpoint, a function signature, or a protocol definition. It has inputs (the task description, the context, the constraints), a contract (what the output should look like), and failure modes (what happens when the input is ambiguous or outside scope). The difference is that most engineers would never ship an API endpoint without documentation, testing, and versioning. They ship prompts like that every day.

A well-structured prompt has distinct, identifiable sections that each serve a specific purpose. Not every prompt needs every section, but understanding the anatomy helps you design deliberately rather than by accumulation. Here are the components that matter:

Role and context. What is the model acting as, and what does it need to know about the situation? This is not just "you are a helpful assistant." It is a specific framing that shapes how the model approaches the task. "You are a senior tax accountant reviewing a client's estimated quarterly payments" produces different output than "you are a financial advisor." The specificity of the role determines the specificity of the reasoning. Vague roles produce vague outputs.

Task definition. What exactly should the model do? The precision of this section determines how reliably the model delivers what you need. "Summarize this document" is ambiguous. Summarize for whom? At what length? Emphasizing what aspects? "Write a three-sentence summary for a non-technical executive, focusing on financial impact and timeline" is a task definition. The difference in output quality between these two instructions is substantial, and it costs nothing but clarity to get the better version.

Input specification. What data is the model working with, and how should it interpret that data? If you are providing a document, tell the model what kind of document it is. If you are providing structured data, explain the schema. If there are fields that might be confusing or empty, address that. The model cannot ask for clarification. Every ambiguity you leave unresolved is an ambiguity the model will resolve on its own, and its resolution may not match yours.

Output specification. What should the output look like? This is the section most prompts lack entirely, and its absence is the single most common cause of inconsistent output. We will address this in detail in the next section.

Constraints and guardrails. What should the model not do? What topics should it avoid? What assumptions should it not make? Constraints are often more important than instructions, because they bound the space of acceptable outputs. A model without constraints will use the full space of what it considers reasonable, which is often broader than what you consider acceptable.

Examples. Concrete input-output pairs that demonstrate what good looks like. Examples are the most efficient way to communicate complex or subtle requirements. A single well-chosen example can encode more information about your expectations than a paragraph of instructions. Two or three examples that show variation across the expected input range are even better. If your prompt does not include examples, you are relying entirely on the model's interpretation of your prose instructions, which is a less reliable communication channel.

The point is not that every prompt needs to be a ten-page document. Simple tasks need simple prompts. The point is that a prompt should be as complete as the task requires, and that completeness should be deliberate. A prompt that is short because the task is simple is good. A prompt that is short because the engineer did not think through the anatomy is a bug.

To make this concrete, consider the difference between two prompts for the same task: classifying customer feedback into categories.

The first prompt says: "Classify the following customer feedback into the appropriate category." This is what most teams start with. It works in demos. The model is smart enough to infer reasonable categories and produce plausible classifications. The problem is that "reasonable" and "plausible" are not engineering standards. This prompt has no defined categories, so the model might invent different ones on different calls. It has no output format, so one call might return "Billing" and another might return "This feedback falls into the billing category." It has no instructions for ambiguous feedback, so the model will guess. It has no role framing, so the model applies generic reasoning rather than domain-specific judgment.

The second prompt says: "You are a customer experience analyst for a B2B SaaS company. Classify the following customer feedback into exactly one of these categories: billing, product_bug, feature_request, onboarding, performance, or other. If the feedback could belong to multiple categories, choose the primary concern. If the feedback is unclear or does not fit any category, use other. Respond with only the category label, lowercase, with no additional text." This prompt is longer. It is also testable, consistent, and production-ready. Every design decision is explicit. Every ambiguity has a resolution rule. The downstream code can parse the output reliably because the output contract is defined.

The difference between these two prompts is not creativity or cleverness. It is engineering completeness. The first prompt delegates every decision to the model. The second prompt makes the decisions upfront and delegates only the classification judgment itself. That is what treating a prompt as an interface looks like in practice.

Output Specification

If there is one change that would most improve the quality and reliability of AI systems across the industry, it would be this: every prompt should include an explicit output specification.

An output specification defines what the response should look like. Not just the content, but the structure, format, length, and constraints. It is the contract between the prompt and whatever code needs to consume the output. Without it, the model guesses what format you want, and its guesses are inconsistent.

Consider a prompt that asks the model to extract key information from a support ticket. Without an output spec, you might get a paragraph of prose on one call, a bulleted list on another, and a JSON-like structure on a third. All three might contain the correct information. But if your downstream code expects JSON, two out of three responses break the pipeline. The model was not wrong. It was never told what right looks like.

A good output specification includes several elements. The format: JSON, markdown, plain text, XML, or whatever your system expects. The schema: which fields should be present, what their types are, whether any are optional. Length constraints: maximum word count, maximum number of items, or target range. Handling instructions for missing or ambiguous data: should the model return null, omit the field, or flag it as uncertain?

The output spec should be precise enough that you could write a validator against it. If you can describe the structure well enough for code to verify it, you have described it well enough for the model to produce it. If your output spec is too vague for a validator, it is too vague for the model.

In practice, the most reliable pattern is to provide both a structural specification and an example of a complete, correct output. The specification tells the model the rules. The example shows what the rules look like in action. Together, they eliminate most of the ambiguity that causes format inconsistency.

Output specifications also serve an important function for your engineering team. They document what the prompt is supposed to produce, which makes the prompt testable, reviewable, and maintainable. When a new engineer reads a prompt with a clear output spec, they understand immediately what the prompt does and what success looks like. When they read a prompt without one, they have to run it several times and infer the expected output from observation. The output spec is documentation that also improves model performance. There is no reason not to include one.

A failure pattern I see regularly: the gap between what the model produces and what the code expects grows silently over time. A prompt is written. It produces output in a particular format. Code is written to parse that format. The prompt is later modified, subtly changing the output format. The parsing code is not updated. For a while, the system works because the change is minor and the parser is flexible. Then one day the accumulated drift crosses a threshold and the parser breaks. If the prompt had an explicit output spec, and the spec was tested automatically, this drift would have been caught immediately. Without the spec, the drift accumulates until it causes a production failure.

Treat the output spec as a shared contract between the person who writes the prompt and the person who writes the code that consumes the output. Both sides should reference the same spec. When the spec changes, both sides should update. This is the same discipline as maintaining API documentation between a service and its consumers. The only difference is that one side of the interface is a model instead of a function.

Edge Case Handling in Prompts

Most prompts are designed for the average case. The typical input. The happy path. And on those inputs, most prompts work reasonably well, because the average case is what the model handles most naturally. The test of a prompt's quality is not how it performs on the average case. It is how it performs on the edges.

Edge cases in AI prompting come in several forms.

Missing or incomplete input. What happens when a required field is empty? When the document the model is supposed to summarize is blank? When the user asks a question that the retrieved context does not actually address? If your prompt does not include explicit instructions for these scenarios, the model will improvise. Sometimes it will improvise well. Sometimes it will hallucinate an answer. Sometimes it will produce a generic response that is technically not wrong but is useless. The only way to get consistent, reliable behavior on missing inputs is to tell the model what to do about them.

Ambiguous input. What happens when the user's question could be interpreted in multiple ways? When a name matches multiple records? When the context contains conflicting information? Ambiguity is the breeding ground for inconsistent outputs. A model without guidance will pick an interpretation, and different invocations may pick different interpretations for the same input. If your prompt instructs the model to identify ambiguity and either ask for clarification or flag the ambiguity in its response, you get predictable behavior instead of random resolution.

Adversarial or out-of-scope input. What happens when a user tries to get the model to do something outside its intended scope? When they submit a support ticket that is actually a request for the model to write a poem? When they attempt prompt injection, embedding instructions in the input data that try to override the system prompt? Your prompt should include explicit boundaries: what the model should refuse, how it should refuse, and what it should do instead. The model's default refusal behavior is often either too aggressive (refusing legitimate edge cases) or too permissive (following injected instructions). Specifying refusal behavior explicitly in the prompt gives you control over this.

Volume and length edge cases. What happens when the input is much longer or much shorter than typical? When the user provides a single word where a paragraph was expected? When they provide a 50-page document where a single page was expected? Your prompt should either specify input constraints or include instructions for how to handle inputs that fall outside the expected range. A model asked to summarize a single word will produce something, but that something is unlikely to be useful. A model told "if the input is fewer than 20 words, respond with: the input is too short to summarize meaningfully" handles the edge case gracefully.

The discipline of edge case handling in prompts mirrors the discipline of edge case handling in code. The difference is that in code, an unhandled edge case produces a clear error. In a prompt, an unhandled edge case produces a response that looks normal but may be wrong, inconsistent, or misleading. The failure is silent, which makes it worse. You cannot rely on the model to tell you it does not know what to do. It will always produce something. Your job is to make sure that "something" is the right behavior, even on inputs you did not design for.

A useful practice: after writing a prompt, spend ten minutes brainstorming the worst inputs it could receive. The shortest input. The longest input. The most ambiguous input. The most adversarial input. An input in the wrong language. An input that contains no useful information. Then, for each of those, decide what the correct behavior should be and add handling for it to the prompt. This exercise consistently reveals gaps that would have surfaced as production issues.

Prompt Versioning

Prompts change. They change because the task requirements evolve. They change because edge cases are discovered. They change because the model updates and the old phrasing no longer produces the same results. They change because someone has an idea for improvement and edits the prompt directly without telling anyone.

That last scenario is the one that causes the most damage, and it happens constantly in teams that do not version their prompts. A prompt that lives as a string in application code, without version history, without change documentation, and without a review process, is a prompt that will be modified in ways that break things. Not because the modifier is careless, but because without context on why the prompt is the way it is, any change risks undoing a fix for a previous issue or introducing a conflict with an existing instruction.

Prompt versioning means three things.

First, prompts live in version control. Not as strings buried in application code, but as first-class artifacts in their own files, with their own commit history, and ideally in a dedicated directory. This makes it possible to see exactly what changed, when, and why. It also makes it easy to search for all prompts in the codebase, which becomes important as the number of prompts grows. A team with forty prompts scattered across twenty files in three services has no practical way to maintain consistency. A team with forty prompts in a single directory with a shared convention can manage them efficiently.

Second, prompt changes go through review. A pull request for a prompt change should explain what the change does, why it is being made, and what potential side effects were considered. It should include evidence that the change was tested, ideally with before-and-after results on representative inputs. This level of rigor feels excessive to teams accustomed to treating prompts as informal text. It stops feeling excessive after the first time an unreviewed prompt change degrades production quality and nobody knows what changed.

Third, prompt versions are linked to evaluations. When you run your eval suite, the results should be tagged with the prompt version that produced them. This lets you track quality over time and correlate changes in quality with specific prompt modifications. If version 12 of a prompt scores 91 percent on your eval and version 13 scores 85 percent, you know exactly where to look. Without version tagging, all you know is that quality dropped somewhere, sometime, for some reason.

Versioning is also the foundation for one of the most effective prompt improvement strategies: systematic A/B testing. If you can run two prompt versions simultaneously on equivalent traffic and compare their output quality, you can make data-driven decisions about which version is better. This requires version control as infrastructure, not just as a practice. You need to be able to deploy a specific prompt version, route traffic to it, and measure its performance independently.

Let me share a scenario that illustrates why this matters. A team managing an AI-powered report generation system had a prompt that produced quality reports for their standard use case. An engineer noticed that the model sometimes included irrelevant recommendations in the report and added a constraint: "Do not include recommendations that are not directly supported by the data provided." This was a sensible change. It was not reviewed. It was committed directly to the codebase.

The constraint worked for the cases that motivated it. But it also caused the model to become more conservative across the board, suppressing recommendations that were well-supported but that the model now second-guessed because the new instruction made it cautious about what counted as "directly supported." Report quality, as measured by user satisfaction, dropped by eight percent over the following two weeks. The team investigated the model, the context pipeline, and the retrieval system before someone finally looked at the prompt diff and found the one-line change. The total diagnosis time was about fifteen hours of engineering work.

With proper versioning, this scenario plays out differently. The change goes through review, where someone might catch the overly broad constraint. It runs against the eval suite, which might show the quality dip before deployment. If it does ship, the version tag makes it trivial to identify as the cause when quality drops. Fifteen hours of diagnosis becomes fifteen minutes. That is the return on investment for prompt versioning, and it comes not from preventing mistakes, but from making mistakes cheap and fast to diagnose.

Testing Prompts Systematically

Chapter 2 established that testing probabilistic systems requires a different approach than testing deterministic ones. That principle applies directly to prompt testing. You cannot write a test that asserts a specific expected output and expect it to be stable. You need to test for properties, patterns, and quality thresholds rather than exact matches.

A prompt testing strategy has three tiers.

Tier one: structural validation. Does the output conform to the specified format? If the output spec says JSON, is the output valid JSON? If it says the response should contain specific fields, are those fields present? Structural tests are deterministic even when the content is not, because they test the output format rather than the output content. They are fast to write, fast to run, and catch the most common class of prompt failure. Every prompt with an output spec should have structural tests.

Tier two: property-based testing. Does the output satisfy required properties? If the prompt asks for a summary, is the output shorter than the input? If it asks for a sentiment classification, is the output one of the allowed categories? If it asks for a date extraction, does the output contain valid dates? Property tests check that the output falls within the space of acceptable responses without requiring an exact match. They are more meaningful than structural tests and still stable across model updates, because the properties being tested are defined by the task, not by the model's phrasing.

Tier three: quality evaluation. Does the output meet the quality bar for production use? This is where evaluation datasets and scoring rubrics come in, which Chapter 9 covers in depth. Quality evaluation typically involves running the prompt against a set of representative inputs and scoring the outputs against defined criteria, either with automated scoring, human review, or an LLM-as-judge pattern. The results produce a quality score that you track over time. This tier is the most expensive and the most informative. It tells you not just whether the prompt works, but how well it works and whether it is getting better or worse.

The three tiers are additive, not alternatives. Structural tests run on every change, catching format regressions instantly. Property tests run on a broader set of inputs, catching behavioral regressions. Quality evaluations run periodically or on significant changes, providing the deepest assessment. Together, they give you a testing infrastructure that is proportional to the risk and cost of prompt failures in your system.

One practical note: prompt tests should run against the actual model, not a mock. Mocking the model defeats the purpose, because the entire point is to verify that the prompt produces acceptable output from a real, probabilistic system. This means prompt tests are slower and more expensive than typical unit tests. That is the cost of testing probabilistic systems, and it is a cost worth paying. The alternative is discovering prompt failures through user reports, which is slower and more expensive in every way that matters.

Teams that resist investing in prompt testing usually cite the cost: model API calls are expensive, tests are slow, results are non-deterministic so you get flaky test runs. These are real costs, but they need to be compared against the cost of not testing. An untested prompt that produces incorrect output for two percent of users costs you user trust, support tickets, engineering time for emergency fixes, and in some domains, legal or compliance exposure. The testing cost is predictable, bounded, and paid on your schedule. The not-testing cost is unpredictable, unbounded, and paid on the user's schedule, which is always the worst time.

A reasonable starting point if you have no prompt testing today: pick the three prompts in your system that are highest-risk, either because they affect the most users or because incorrect output is most costly. For each one, write five structural tests and five property tests. Run them against the current prompt and establish a baseline. Then run them whenever the prompt changes. This is two days of work at most, and it gives you meaningful coverage on the prompts that matter most. You can expand from there as the practice matures.

Engineering Heuristics

Heuristic 1: A prompt without an output spec is an incomplete interface.

If your prompt does not define what the output should look like, the model will decide for you, and it will decide differently on different invocations. Every prompt that produces output consumed by code, which is most prompts in production, needs an explicit output specification: format, schema, length constraints, and handling instructions for edge cases. If you can write a validator against the spec, it is precise enough. If you cannot, it is too vague. Treat the output spec as mandatory, not optional. It is the contract between the prompt and the rest of your system.

Heuristic 2: Write prompts for the edge case, not the average case.

The average case works with minimal effort. The edge cases are where your prompt's quality is tested. After writing a prompt, spend ten minutes generating the worst plausible inputs: empty input, ambiguous input, adversarial input, input in the wrong format, input that is dramatically longer or shorter than expected. For each, define the correct behavior and encode it in the prompt. This exercise takes minutes and prevents production issues that take hours to diagnose and fix. A prompt that handles edge cases gracefully is a prompt that can be trusted in production. A prompt that was only tested on the happy path is a liability.

Heuristic 3: If you would not ship undocumented code, do not ship undocumented prompts.

A prompt in production should be documented: what it does, what inputs it expects, what output it produces, what edge cases it handles, and what assumptions it makes. This documentation can live as comments within the prompt file, as an accompanying document, or as structured metadata, but it must exist. Prompts without documentation become black boxes within weeks. Nobody remembers why a specific instruction was added. Nobody knows what happens if a clause is removed. The prompt becomes untouchable, and untouchable code is the most expensive code in any codebase. Document the intent, not just the text. The text will change. The intent should survive those changes.

Prompts are interfaces, and they deserve the same engineering discipline as any other interface in your system. They should be structured deliberately, specified clearly, tested systematically, versioned carefully, and documented thoroughly. The craft skill of finding good phrasings is real, but it is a small part of the picture. The larger part is the engineering infrastructure that makes prompts reliable, maintainable, and improvable over time.

Notice how the principles connect back through the book's argument. In Chapter 1, we said the model is not the product. The product layer is. Prompts are a core component of that product layer. In Chapters 3 and 4, we said context is architecture and curation matters. The prompt is the frame around that curated context, the instructions that tell the model how to use what it has been given. A well-designed prompt on top of well-curated context is the combination that produces reliable, high-quality output. Either one alone is insufficient.

This chapter treated prompts as individual units. But in practice, many tasks are too complex for a single prompt to handle well. When a single prompt tries to do too much, it becomes monolithic: hard to test, hard to debug, brittle to change. The next chapter addresses the solution: composability. Breaking complex prompt logic into focused, modular pieces that can be assembled, tested, and evolved independently is the subject of Chapter 6.

Composability Over Complexity

Part III: Prompting

Long, monolithic prompts are hard to debug and brittle to change. The better pattern is to break prompts into focused, composable units that can be assembled and reasoned about independently.

Modular Prompt Design

Every codebase has its version of the God Object: the single class or module that does everything, knows everything, and is impossible to change without breaking something. It starts small. Someone adds a feature. Someone else adds a conditional. A third person adds a special case. Over months, the module accretes logic until it is hundreds or thousands of lines long, no one fully understands it, and every change requires regression testing the entire surface area.

Monolithic prompts follow the same trajectory. A prompt starts as a clean, focused instruction. Then someone adds handling for a new input type. Then someone adds an output format requirement. Then someone adds a constraint for a specific edge case. Then someone adds a few-shot example to correct a behavioral drift. Within a few months, the prompt is a wall of text that mixes role definition, task instructions, format requirements, edge case handling, examples, and behavioral constraints in no particular order. Nobody on the team can explain what removing any given sentence would do, so nothing gets removed. The prompt only grows.

This is the monolith problem, and the solution is the same in prompts as it is in code: decomposition. Break the monolith into smaller, focused units, each with a single responsibility, each testable in isolation, each modifiable without affecting the others.

Modular prompt design means structuring your prompt system so that distinct concerns are handled by distinct prompt components. Instead of one prompt that classifies a support ticket, extracts key entities, determines urgency, drafts a response, and selects a routing destination, you have five prompts: one for classification, one for entity extraction, one for urgency scoring, one for response drafting, and one for routing. Each prompt is focused. Each has a clear input and output contract. Each can be tested, improved, and debugged independently.

The objection I hear most often is that this means more API calls, which means more cost and more latency. This is true. Modular prompts do involve more calls than a monolithic prompt. But the trade-off almost always favors modularity for systems that need to be maintained over time. A monolithic prompt that is 10 percent cheaper per request but takes three days to debug and a week to modify safely is more expensive than five modular prompts that cost more per request but can be debugged in an hour and modified in an afternoon. Engineering time is more expensive than API tokens for any team building a product that will exist for more than a few months.

There is also a quality argument for modularity that goes beyond maintainability. Models perform better on focused tasks than on compound tasks. A prompt that asks the model to do one thing well produces more reliable output than a prompt that asks it to do five things in sequence. Each additional task in a monolithic prompt increases the probability that the model will cut corners on one of them, especially the tasks in the middle, which receive less attention than the tasks at the beginning and end. Splitting compound tasks into focused prompts does not just make the system easier to maintain. It makes each individual task more reliable.

Let me make this concrete. A team I worked with had a monolithic prompt for processing job applications. The prompt asked the model to: parse the resume, extract key qualifications, compare qualifications against the job requirements, score the match on a 1-10 scale, identify any disqualifying criteria, and generate a summary paragraph explaining the score. All in one prompt. The prompt was over 2,000 tokens of instructions, and it worked adequately about 75 percent of the time. The other 25 percent, it would skip the disqualification check, produce inconsistent scoring, or generate summaries that contradicted the score.

They decomposed it into four prompts. Prompt one: parse the resume and extract qualifications in a structured format. Prompt two: compare the extracted qualifications against the job requirements and produce a match report. Prompt three: evaluate the match report for disqualifying criteria and assign a score. Prompt four: generate the summary from the match report and score. Each prompt was under 500 tokens of instructions. Each had its own test suite. Accuracy on the full pipeline went from 75 percent to 93 percent, and the 7 percent of failures were now traceable to a specific step rather than hiding somewhere in a 2,000-token monolith.

The cost was four API calls instead of one. The latency was roughly double because the calls ran sequentially. But the total token cost was actually lower, because each focused prompt used less context than the monolith, and the overall quality improvement meant fewer outputs needed manual correction. The trade-off was clearly favorable, and it improved further as the team optimized individual steps over the following weeks, something that would have been impractical with the monolith.

Prompt Chaining

Prompt chaining is the pattern of connecting multiple prompts in sequence, where the output of one prompt becomes part of the input to the next. It is the primary mechanism for implementing modular prompt design. Instead of a single prompt doing everything, a chain of prompts handles complex tasks step by step, with each step building on the results of the previous one.

The simplest chain is linear: prompt A produces output that feeds into prompt B, which produces output that feeds into prompt C. A document analysis pipeline might work this way. Step one: extract key facts from the document. Step two: classify the document based on the extracted facts. Step three: generate a summary tailored to the document's classification. Each step has a focused task, a clear input, and a clear output. The chain as a whole performs a complex analysis that no single prompt could do as reliably.

More complex chains include branching logic. The output of one step determines which subsequent prompt to run. A customer inquiry pipeline might classify the inquiry first, then branch: billing questions go to one prompt, technical issues go to another, feature requests go to a third. Each branch is optimized for its specific task, with its own context, its own examples, and its own output format. The classification step at the top routes traffic efficiently, and each branch handles its domain well because it is not trying to handle every domain.

Chains can also include validation and retry loops. After a generation step, a validation step checks whether the output conforms to the required schema and quality criteria. If it does not, the chain either retries the generation step with additional guidance or routes to a fallback path. This pattern is particularly useful for tasks where output format matters, like JSON generation. The generation prompt produces the content. The validation step confirms structure. If validation fails, a retry prompt that includes the error message and the original output asks the model to fix the specific issue. This is more reliable than hoping the generation prompt gets the format right on the first try.

The key design principle for chains is that each link should have an explicit contract: what input it accepts, what output it produces, and what constitutes valid output. These contracts are how you test, debug, and monitor the chain. If the final output is wrong, you inspect each link's output to find where the problem originated. Without contracts at each step, debugging a chain is like debugging a pipeline where no intermediate values are logged. The problem could be anywhere, and you have no way to narrow it down.

A practical implementation pattern: every prompt in a chain should be callable independently with representative test inputs. You should be able to take the classification prompt, run it against twenty test inputs, and verify that the classifications are correct, without running the full chain. This property, independent testability, is what makes chains debuggable and maintainable. If a prompt only works in the context of the full chain and cannot be tested alone, it is too tightly coupled to the other steps.

One often-overlooked design opportunity in chains is parallelism. Not every step needs to wait for the previous step to finish. If your pipeline includes a classification step and an entity extraction step that are both based on the original input and do not depend on each other, they can run in parallel. A document processing pipeline might run metadata extraction, content summarization, and key term extraction simultaneously, then merge the results into a final analysis step. Parallelism reduces total latency without sacrificing modularity. The trade-off is slightly more complex orchestration code, but any team comfortable with async programming will find it straightforward.

Error handling in chains deserves explicit attention. What happens when one step in the chain fails? If step two produces malformed output, step three receives bad input and its output is unreliable, and this propagates through every subsequent step. The default behavior, which is to let failures cascade silently, is the worst option. A better design includes validation between steps: check the output of each step against its contract before passing it to the next step. If validation fails, you have several options depending on the situation. Retry the failed step with a modified prompt that includes the error. Skip the step and use a default value. Route to a fallback path that handles the degraded case. Abort the chain and return an honest error to the user. Each option is appropriate in different circumstances, but the key point is that the choice should be explicit and designed, not left to whatever happens when the next step receives garbage input.

Separation of Concerns in Prompts

Separation of concerns is one of the oldest principles in software engineering, and it applies to prompts with equal force. The idea is simple: each component should handle one concern and handle it well. When concerns are mixed, changes to one concern risk breaking another, and the resulting system is harder to understand, test, and evolve.

In prompt design, the concerns that should be separated include:

Task logic vs. output formatting. The instructions that tell the model what to do (analyze sentiment, extract entities, generate a summary) are a different concern than the instructions that tell the model how to format the result (as JSON, as a bulleted list, within a word count). Mixing these makes it hard to change one without affecting the other. If you want to change your output format from JSON to XML, you should be able to do that without touching the task instructions. If the two are interleaved in a single prompt, every formatting change risks destabilizing the task logic.

Domain knowledge vs. behavioral rules. Domain knowledge is the specific information the model needs to do its job: the categories for classification, the criteria for scoring, the definitions of key terms. Behavioral rules are the constraints on how the model should behave: what tone to use, when to refuse, how to handle ambiguity. These change at different rates and for different reasons. Domain knowledge changes when the business changes. Behavioral rules change when the user experience changes. Mixing them means every business change risks affecting behavior, and every behavior change risks affecting domain accuracy.

Core instructions vs. edge case handling. The instructions for the typical case are the backbone of your prompt. The instructions for edge cases are important but should not clutter the core flow. When edge case instructions are mixed into the main body of the prompt, they add length and complexity that the model must process on every request, even when the edge case does not apply. A better pattern is to handle edge cases through branching in the chain (detect the edge case with a lightweight check, then route to a specialized prompt) or through a clearly delineated section of the prompt that the model can recognize as conditional handling.

Static instructions vs. dynamic content. This echoes the context architecture discussion from Chapter 3. Static instructions that apply to every request should be clearly separated from dynamic content that varies per request. When these are interleaved, it becomes difficult to modify the static instructions without affecting how the dynamic content is processed, and vice versa. Clean separation also makes it easier to version and test the static instructions independently, which is essential for the prompt versioning discipline described in Chapter 5.

The practical test for whether concerns are properly separated: can you change one concern without touching the others? If changing the output format requires editing the task instructions, the concerns are coupled. If adding a new edge case requires modifying the core instructions, the concerns are coupled. Decoupling takes deliberate design work, but it pays off every time you need to make a change, which in a production AI system is frequently.

A useful exercise: take your most complex prompt and highlight each sentence in a different color based on which concern it addresses. Task logic in one color. Formatting in another. Behavioral rules in a third. Edge case handling in a fourth. If the colors are interleaved throughout the prompt, the concerns are mixed. If they form distinct blocks, the separation is cleaner. This is a diagnostic exercise, not a formatting rule. The colors show you where the coupling is, and that tells you where to decompose first.

Reusability and Shared Libraries

As the number of prompts in your system grows, you will notice patterns. Multiple prompts share the same output formatting instructions. Multiple prompts use the same tone and behavioral guidelines. Multiple prompts include the same safety constraints. If each prompt defines these independently, you end up with duplicated text that drifts over time as different engineers modify different copies.

The solution is the same as in code: extract shared patterns into reusable components. A shared prompt library is a collection of prompt fragments that can be composed into complete prompts. A formatting module that defines your standard JSON output structure. A behavioral module that defines your tone, safety, and refusal guidelines. A domain module that defines the classification categories for a specific business area.

Implementing this is straightforward. Most teams use a template system: prompts are assembled from named fragments at runtime. The system prompt might be composed of a base behavioral template, a feature-specific task template, and a dynamic section populated per request. Each template is versioned, tested, and maintained in a single location. Changes to the behavioral template propagate to every prompt that uses it, which is exactly what you want when you update a global policy like tone guidelines or safety constraints.

The benefits mirror the benefits of shared libraries in code. Consistency: every prompt that uses the formatting module produces output in the same format. Maintainability: updating the format in one place updates it everywhere. Reduced duplication: no more copying and pasting the same instructions across dozens of prompts. Discoverability: new engineers can browse the library to understand what building blocks are available before writing a new prompt from scratch.

The consistency benefit deserves special emphasis. I have seen systems where twelve different prompts each defined their own version of the same safety instructions. Over time, the versions diverged. Some included a newer constraint. Some used outdated language. One had a copy-paste error that accidentally removed a key clause. When an audit revealed the inconsistency, reconciling the twelve versions took a full engineering day. If the safety instructions had lived in a shared template from the start, the issue would not have existed. Changes would propagate automatically, and the audit would have been a single file review.

There is a risk to watch for: over-abstraction. If your template system becomes so modular that understanding a single prompt requires tracing through seven template fragments, you have traded one kind of complexity for another. The goal is shared building blocks, not a dependency graph that requires a diagram to understand. A good rule of thumb: if a prompt cannot be fully assembled and read as a coherent document in a single view, the template structure is too fragmented. The final assembled prompt should always be human-readable, because the human-readable version is what the model sees.

One particularly effective pattern: maintain a "prompt registry" that catalogs every prompt in your system with metadata about what it does, what templates it uses, what inputs it expects, and where it is used. This registry becomes invaluable as the system scales. When someone needs to add a new feature, they check the registry first to see if a similar prompt already exists or if existing components can be reused. When a template changes, the registry shows every prompt that will be affected. When debugging, the registry provides the map of the system that is otherwise only in people's heads.

Debugging Composed Prompts

Composed systems are easier to debug than monolithic ones, but only if you build the debugging infrastructure alongside the system. Without it, a chain of five prompts can actually be harder to debug than a single monolithic prompt, because the failure could originate at any step and propagate through the rest.

The single most important debugging capability for composed prompts is intermediate output logging. Every step in a chain should log its full input, its full output, and relevant metadata like the prompt version, the model used, and the latency. When a final output is wrong, you trace backwards through the chain, inspecting each step's output, until you find the step where the output diverged from what was expected. This is the AI equivalent of adding print statements to a pipeline, and it is equally essential.

Without intermediate logging, debugging a chain looks like this: the final output is wrong, you stare at the final prompt and the final input, you cannot figure out what went wrong, you add logging, you reproduce the issue, and then you find the bug. With intermediate logging from the start, debugging looks like this: the final output is wrong, you pull the logs, you see that step three produced an incorrect classification, you inspect step three's input and prompt, you find the issue. The difference is hours versus minutes, and it compounds as the chain gets longer.

A second important capability is step-level evaluation. If each prompt in a chain has its own test suite (as recommended in the modular design section), you can run those tests periodically to detect degradation at individual steps before it surfaces as a failure in the full chain. If step two's classification accuracy drops from 94 to 88 percent, you will see it in step two's eval results even if the end-to-end chain has not visibly broken yet, because the downstream steps are compensating or the drop has not crossed the failure threshold. Catching problems at the step level, before they compound through the chain, is always cheaper and faster than catching them at the output level.

A third capability that becomes valuable at scale: chain-level tracing. This is the practice of assigning a trace ID to each request and propagating it through every step of the chain. With tracing, you can reconstruct the complete history of any request: what went in at each step, what came out, how long each step took, and which prompt version was active. This is operationally identical to distributed tracing in a microservices architecture, and it serves the same purpose. When you need to understand why a specific request produced a specific output, the trace gives you the complete picture.

The investment in debugging infrastructure should be proportional to the complexity of the chain. A two-step chain can get by with basic logging. A five-step chain with branching and retry logic needs intermediate logging, step-level evaluation, and tracing. The cost of building this infrastructure upfront is significantly lower than the cost of building it under pressure during an incident, which is when you will wish you had it.

There is a cultural point here worth making. Teams that invest in debugging infrastructure for their prompt chains develop a different relationship with failures. Failures stop being scary and start being diagnostic. When something goes wrong, the conversation is not "the AI is broken" but rather "step three's classification is drifting on inputs with ambiguous language, let's look at the eval data." That shift, from vague alarm to specific diagnosis, is the mark of a mature AI engineering team. And it is only possible when the composed system is observable at every layer.

Engineering Heuristics

Heuristic 1: If you cannot explain what a prompt section does in one sentence, split it.

This is the readability test. Every section of a prompt, and every prompt in a chain, should have a purpose that can be stated in a single sentence. "This section defines the output format." "This prompt extracts entities from the input." "This step validates the JSON structure." If you find yourself needing a paragraph to explain what a section does, it is handling multiple concerns and should be decomposed. The one-sentence test is not about brevity. It is about clarity of purpose. A prompt component with a clear purpose is testable, modifiable, and debuggable. A prompt component with a murky purpose is none of those things.

Heuristic 2: Prefer chained focused prompts over one omnibus prompt.

When a task involves multiple distinct operations, classification plus extraction plus generation for example, the default should be to implement it as a chain of focused prompts rather than a single prompt that does everything. The monolithic prompt will work in demos. It will struggle in production, where inputs are messier, edge cases are more varied, and the cost of debugging is real. A chain gives you isolation, where a failure in one step does not corrupt the others. It gives you testability, where each step can be evaluated independently. It gives you flexibility, where you can improve one step without risking the others. The additional cost in API calls and latency is real, but for most production systems it is a better trade-off than the maintenance cost of a monolith.

Heuristic 3: Build a shared prompt library before writing duplicates.

Before you write a new prompt that includes behavioral guidelines, output formatting instructions, or domain definitions that already exist in another prompt, extract those shared components into a reusable library. The second time you reach for the same block of text is the right time to extract it. Not the first time, which is premature abstraction. Not the fifth time, which means you already have five copies drifting apart. Build the shared library early, keep it discoverable, and make it the default starting point for new prompts. The library does not need to be complex. A directory of named text fragments with a simple composition mechanism is enough. What matters is that shared concerns are defined once and used everywhere.

Chapters 5 and 6 form the prompting pair. Chapter 5 treated the prompt as an interface, subject to the same engineering discipline as any other interface in your system. This chapter addressed what happens when a single interface is not enough: you decompose, you chain, you compose, and you build the infrastructure to maintain and debug the result.

Together, Parts I through III have established the conceptual foundations (how to think about AI systems), the context discipline (what to feed the model), and the prompting discipline (how to instruct the model). The next part of the book turns to a different challenge entirely: what happens when the system acts on its own. Part IV opens with Chapter 7,

Scope Before Autonomy, which addresses the most consequential and most frequently mishandled question in agentic AI: how much freedom to give the system, and how to bound it safely.

Scope Before Autonomy

Part IV: Agents

The biggest mistake teams make with agentic AI is giving it too much room too soon. Autonomy needs clear boundaries to function safely and predictably. Define exactly what an agent can and cannot do before deciding how much it can act on its own.

Defining Agent Scope

The word "agent" has become one of the most overloaded terms in AI. It gets applied to everything from a chatbot that can call a search API to a fully autonomous system that can write code, deploy infrastructure, and manage production databases. The range of what people mean by "agent" is so broad that the word itself has become almost useless for engineering discussions. For the purposes of this chapter, an agent is any AI system that can take actions in the world beyond generating text. It can call APIs. It can read and write data. It can trigger workflows. It can interact with external systems. The defining characteristic is that it does things, not just says things.

That distinction matters enormously, because a system that does things can do the wrong things. A chatbot that generates an incorrect response is annoying. An agent that executes an incorrect action, sending the wrong email, deleting the wrong record, deploying the wrong configuration, has real-world consequences that are much harder to undo. The stakes of getting it right are categorically different when the system acts rather than advises.

This is why scope comes before autonomy. Before you decide how much freedom to give an agent, you need to define the boundaries of what it is allowed to do at all. Scope is the set of actions the agent can take, the data it can access, the systems it can interact with, and the conditions under which it should operate. Autonomy is how independently it operates within that scope. Getting the order wrong, deciding how autonomous the agent should be before defining what it should be autonomous about, is the most common and most expensive mistake teams make with agentic systems.

The temptation to skip scoping is strong. The technology demos are compelling. An agent that can browse the web, write code, interact with APIs, and chain together complex multi-step workflows looks incredibly powerful. And it is. But power without boundaries is liability. An agent that can do anything can do the wrong thing with the same efficiency it does the right thing. The question is not "what can this agent do?" It is "what should this agent be allowed to do, given the consequences of getting it wrong?"

Scope definition starts with a simple exercise that I recommend every team run before building any agentic feature: write down every action the agent should be able to take, every data source it should be able to access, and every system it should be able to interact with. Then, critically, write down every action it should not be able to take, every data source it should not access, and every system it should not touch. The second list is more important than the first. The first list defines capability. The second list defines safety.

Most teams I have worked with can produce the first list easily. They struggle with the second list, because it requires thinking about everything the system could do wrong, not just everything it should do right. But that difficulty is precisely why the exercise matters. If you cannot articulate what the agent should not do, you have not thought deeply enough about the failure modes. And if you have not thought about the failure modes, you will discover them in production.

To put this in terms that connect back to earlier chapters: scope definition is the agent-layer equivalent of the output specification from Chapter 5. An output specification defines what the prompt should produce. A scope definition defines what the agent should do. Both serve the same purpose: converting an implicit, assumed boundary into an explicit, testable one. And both suffer from the same failure mode when omitted: the system fills in the blanks on its own, and its choices may not match yours.

There is a practical tension that every team building agentic features faces: narrow scope means fewer capabilities, which can mean a less impressive product. The urge to widen the scope, to let the agent do more so the demo is more impressive or the user experience is more seamless, is constant. This is where engineering discipline matters most. The right question is not "what would be cool?" It is "what can we scope tightly enough to deploy with confidence?" An agent that does three things reliably is more valuable than an agent that does ten things unpredictably. Users learn to distrust unreliable agents quickly, and regaining that trust is far harder than earning it with a focused, reliable feature in the first place.

Tool Boundaries and Access Control

In most agentic frameworks, the agent's capabilities are defined by its tools: the functions, APIs, and interfaces it can call. Tool design is scope design. Every tool you give the agent expands its capability surface, and with it, its failure surface. The principle is straightforward: give the agent the minimum set of tools it needs to accomplish its task, and nothing more.

This is the principle of least privilege applied to AI agents, and it is just as important here as it is in traditional security engineering. In security, least privilege means a service account should have only the permissions required for its function. In agentic AI, least privilege means the agent should have access to only the tools required for its task. An agent whose job is to summarize customer support tickets does not need access to the billing API. An agent that drafts marketing copy does not need access to the production database. These sound obvious in isolation, but in practice, agents accumulate tools the same way monolithic prompts accumulate instructions: gradually, one "it might be useful" addition at a time, until the tool surface is far broader than the task requires.

Tool design should follow the same interface discipline described in Chapter 5. Each tool should have a clear name that describes what it does, a clear description of when to use it, defined input parameters, and a defined output format. The descriptions matter more than you might expect, because the agent decides which tools to use based on those descriptions. A vague tool description leads to the agent using the tool in situations it was not designed for. A precise description constrains the agent's tool selection to appropriate contexts.

Beyond tool selection, access control within tools matters. If the agent has a tool that queries a database, what tables can it query? What columns can it see? Can it only read, or can it also write? Can it run arbitrary queries, or only parameterized queries from a predefined set? Each of these decisions narrows the scope and reduces the potential for harm. A database tool that only runs predefined read queries from a whitelist is fundamentally safer than a database tool that accepts arbitrary SQL. The agent's capability is reduced, but so is its ability to cause damage. That trade-off almost always favors safety.

A useful implementation pattern: wrap every tool in a permissions layer that is separate from the tool's logic. The tool itself does the work. The permissions layer checks whether the agent is allowed to invoke the tool in this context, with these parameters, for this user. This separation makes it possible to change permissions without changing tool logic, to audit permissions independently, and to enforce consistent access control across all tools even as new tools are added. It is the same pattern as middleware in a web application, and it serves the same purpose: centralizing a cross-cutting concern that would otherwise be scattered across every individual component.

Let me illustrate why tool boundary design matters with a scenario I encountered. A team built an agent for managing internal IT support requests. The agent could create tickets, update ticket status, look up employee information, and send Slack messages to notify employees about their ticket status. These were the intended tools. During testing, the team noticed the agent occasionally looked up employee information for people unrelated to the current ticket, apparently to gather context that it thought might be useful. The lookups were harmless in testing but raised a serious concern: in production, with real employee data, an agent doing speculative lookups across the employee directory is a privacy issue.

The fix was to add a constraint to the employee lookup tool: it could only be called with the employee ID associated with the current ticket. The tool still worked. Its interface was unchanged. But its scope was narrowed from "look up any employee" to "look up the employee relevant to this ticket." That single constraint eliminated an entire category of unintended behavior. This is what thoughtful tool boundary design looks like: not removing capability, but channeling it so the agent can do its job without wandering into areas it has no reason to access.

Trust Levels and Permissions

Not all actions carry the same risk. Reading a customer's order history is low-risk. Modifying a customer's order is medium-risk. Issuing a refund is high-risk. Deleting an account is very high-risk. The agent's permissions should reflect this risk gradient, and the autonomy granted at each level should be calibrated to the consequences of getting it wrong.

A trust level framework is a practical way to implement this. Define three or four trust levels, each with a different permission set and a different autonomy model. The exact levels depend on your domain, but a common structure looks like this:

Level 1: Read-only. The agent can access information and generate responses, but it cannot modify any data or trigger any actions. This is the safest level, appropriate for informational features where the agent answers questions or provides analysis. The failure mode at this level is limited to incorrect information, which is bad but recoverable. Most agentic features should start at this level and prove reliability before being promoted.

Level 2: Reversible actions. The agent can take actions that are easily undone: creating draft documents, sending internal notifications, tagging records, adding items to a queue for human review. The failure mode at this level includes incorrect actions, but the damage is limited because the actions can be reversed without significant cost. This is the level where most agents deliver meaningful productivity value, because they are doing real work but with a safety net.

Level 3: Consequential actions with confirmation. The agent can take actions with real-world impact, sending external emails, modifying records, making purchases, but only with explicit human confirmation before execution. The agent prepares the action and presents it for approval. The human reviews and authorizes. This level handles the tension between autonomy and safety by giving the agent the intelligence to decide what to do while keeping a human in the loop for the actual execution. Chapter 8 covers the design of these confirmation flows in detail.

Level 4: Autonomous consequential actions. The agent can take consequential actions without human confirmation. This is the highest trust level, and it should be earned through demonstrated reliability, not granted by default. An agent should only operate at Level 4 for specific actions where it has a proven track record: where evaluation data shows consistent accuracy above a defined threshold, where the monitoring infrastructure can detect and alert on failures quickly, and where the cost of a failure is bounded and recoverable. Very few actions in most systems should reach Level 4, and the path to get there should be gradual and evidence-based.

The key insight is that trust levels are not assigned to the agent as a whole. They are assigned per action, per context. An agent might operate at Level 4 for tagging support tickets (low-risk, high confidence) and Level 3 for sending customer emails (higher risk, needs confirmation) within the same session. The trust level should match the risk of the specific action, not the general capability of the agent.

Implementing trust levels requires your tool layer to be aware of them. Each tool call should include metadata about which trust level the action falls into. The orchestration layer checks the trust level before executing: Level 1 and 2 actions proceed automatically. Level 3 actions trigger a confirmation workflow. Level 4 actions proceed automatically but are logged with additional detail for audit purposes. This is not complex to implement, but it needs to be designed upfront rather than retrofitted after the first incident.

A common mistake with trust levels is treating them as a one-time assignment that never changes. In practice, trust should be dynamic. An agent that has been operating reliably at Level 2 for a specific action might earn promotion to Level 3 based on performance data. An agent that encounters a novel input pattern it has not been tested on should temporarily drop to a lower trust level for that interaction. Building this dynamism into the trust framework requires the evaluation and monitoring infrastructure described in Part V, but the architectural decisions to support it should be made here, at design time.

There is also a user-facing dimension to trust levels that affects product design. When an agent takes a Level 2 action (reversible, automatic), should the user see a notification? When it takes a Level 3 action (consequential, requiring confirmation), what should the confirmation experience look like? When it takes a Level 4 action (autonomous, consequential), should the user see a post-action summary? These UX decisions should be tied to the trust levels so that the user experience reflects the actual risk profile of what the agent is doing. An agent that silently takes consequential actions without any user visibility is an agent that will eventually do something the user did not want and that the user did not know about until it was too late.

Scope Creep in Agentic Systems

Scope creep in traditional software is well understood: features get added, boundaries blur, and the system gradually does more than it was designed to do. Scope creep in agentic systems is worse, because it can happen without anyone writing new code.

An agent's effective scope is defined partly by its tools and permissions, and partly by its prompt and the model's own reasoning. Even within well-defined tool boundaries, an agent can find creative ways to use its tools that the designers did not anticipate. An agent with a "send email" tool and a "search customer database" tool might combine them in ways that were not intended, such as searching for all customers in a segment and sending each of them an email based on the agent's own interpretation of an ambiguous instruction. The tools are working as designed. The composition of those tools into an action sequence is where the scope exceeded what was intended.

This is a form of scope creep that is unique to agentic systems, and it is one of the strongest arguments for explicit scoping. The agent's instructions need to define not just what tools are available but what workflows are permitted. "You can use the search tool and the email tool" is insufficient. "You can use the search tool to look up individual customer records when the customer's name or ID is provided, and you can use the email tool to send a single response to the customer currently being served" is a scope definition. The difference is specificity about how the tools should be combined, not just what tools exist.

Scope creep also happens organizationally. A team deploys an agent for a specific use case. It works well. Another team asks if the agent can handle their use case too. Rather than building a separate agent with appropriate scoping, someone expands the existing agent's tools and instructions. Then a third team asks for their use case. The agent's scope grows, its prompt becomes more complex, its tool surface widens, and eventually it is the agentic equivalent of the monolithic prompt from Chapter 6: trying to do too much, doing none of it as well as a focused alternative would, and carrying risk across domains that should be isolated.

The defense against scope creep is the same in agentic systems as it is everywhere else: explicit boundaries, regular audits, and the discipline to say no. Review the agent's tool surface quarterly. Ask whether every tool is still needed. Check whether the agent has been using tools in ways that were not intended. Compare the agent's actual behavior in production against its designed scope. If the two have diverged, tighten the scope. An agent that is doing more than it was designed to do is an agent that is operating outside its tested and evaluated boundaries, which means it is operating in a region where its reliability is unknown.

One concrete practice that helps: maintain a tool usage log that records not just which tools the agent called, but the full context of why it called them. Periodically review a sample of tool calls and ask: was this call within the intended scope? Was the tool used for the purpose it was designed for? Were the parameters within expected ranges? This audit practice catches scope creep before it becomes a problem. It also provides the data you need to make informed decisions about whether the scope should be expanded, based on evidence of the agent's actual behavior rather than assumptions about what it ought to be doing.

Practical Scoping Frameworks

A scoping framework is a structured way to think through and document an agent's boundaries before building it. There are several approaches that work well in practice.

The Action Inventory. Before building, list every action the agent could potentially take. For each action, document: what it does, what data it reads or modifies, what the consequences of an incorrect execution are, and what trust level it requires. This inventory becomes the agent's capability specification. Actions not on the inventory are not permitted, regardless of whether the agent's tools could technically support them. The inventory should be a living document, reviewed and updated as the system evolves, but additions should require the same justification and review as adding a new API endpoint to a production service.

The Blast Radius Analysis. For each action, answer the question: if this action is executed incorrectly, what is the worst that can happen? The answer determines the risk tier and the appropriate trust level. An agent that can tag a support ticket incorrectly has a small blast radius: the ticket goes to the wrong queue and gets rerouted manually. An agent that can issue a refund incorrectly has a larger blast radius: money leaves the company and reclaiming it requires a process. An agent that can delete production data has a very large blast radius. The blast radius should be proportional to the level of oversight, confirmation, and logging applied to that action.

The Negative Scope Document. A document that explicitly lists everything the agent cannot do. This is not a list of features that were considered and rejected. It is a list of actions, data, and systems that the agent is deliberately prohibited from accessing. "The agent cannot access financial data." "The agent cannot send communications to customers outside of the active support thread." "The agent cannot modify or delete records; it can only create and read." The negative scope document serves as both a design constraint and an audit artifact. If the agent is found to be doing something on the prohibited list, it is a defect, not a feature, regardless of whether the action produced a good outcome.

The Progressive Expansion Plan. A roadmap for how the agent's scope will be expanded over time, based on demonstrated performance. Start with the narrowest useful scope. Define the metrics that must be met before the scope is expanded. Specify what the next expansion looks like and what metrics it requires. This prevents the common pattern of launching with a narrow scope and then expanding it reactively based on user requests or leadership pressure, without the evidence to support the expansion. The plan says: "We will expand to Level 3 email sending when the agent achieves 95 percent accuracy on email draft quality for 30 consecutive days." That is an engineering criterion. "We should probably let it send emails now, it seems to be working" is not.

None of these frameworks are novel. They are adaptations of practices from traditional security engineering, operational risk management, and system design. The point is that agentic AI systems need these practices even more than traditional systems do, because the agent's behavior is probabilistic and emergent rather than deterministic and predictable. The tools are familiar. The urgency of applying them is new.

Teams that skip formal scoping tend to follow a predictable arc. They build the agent quickly. The demo is impressive. They ship it. Within the first month, the agent does something unexpected: uses a tool in an unintended way, accesses data it should not have seen, or takes an action that was technically within its permissions but outside its intended purpose. The team scrambles to add constraints, but by then the constraints are reactive patches rather than principled boundaries. The agent becomes harder to reason about because the constraints were added piecemeal rather than designed coherently. Eventually, someone suggests starting over with a clear scoping exercise, which is the exercise they should have done before building the first version.

Starting with scope is not slower. It is faster, because it prevents the rework cycle that unscoped agents invariably produce. An afternoon spent on the Action Inventory and Blast Radius Analysis saves weeks of firefighting later. That is the practical argument for scope before autonomy: it is not just safer, it is more efficient.

Engineering Heuristics

Heuristic 1: Start with the minimum tool surface an agent needs.

When designing an agent, the default should be to include as few tools as possible, not as many. Every tool is a capability, and every capability is a potential failure mode. Start with the tools that are strictly necessary for the core use case. Run the system. Evaluate its performance. Then add tools incrementally, one at a time, with evidence that each addition improves the system and with evaluation that the addition does not introduce new failure modes. The first instinct when an agent underperforms is to give it more tools. Resist that instinct. Often the agent underperforms because its existing tools are poorly designed or its prompt does not guide tool selection well, not because it lacks capability.

Heuristic 2: Scope is a safety property, not just an organizational one.

It is tempting to think of scope as a project management concept: what is in scope, what is out of scope, how to prioritize. In agentic systems, scope is a safety property. An agent operating outside its designed scope is an agent operating in an untested, unevaluated region of behavior. It might work fine. It might cause damage. You do not know, because you did not test for it. Treat scope boundaries with the same seriousness you treat security boundaries. An agent that exceeds its scope should trigger the same kind of alert as a service that exceeds its access permissions. Both represent a system operating outside its designed and tested parameters.

Heuristic 3: If you cannot describe what an agent cannot do, it is under-scoped.

The negative scope test. Ask your team: what is this agent not allowed to do? If the answer is vague or if the team has to think about it, the agent is under-scoped. A well-scoped agent has explicit, documented boundaries that anyone on the team can recite. It cannot access financial data. It cannot send external communications. It cannot modify production records. It cannot run for more than ten steps without human checkpoint. These boundaries should be as concrete and testable as any other system requirement. If you find yourself saying "well, it should not do that, but there is nothing technically preventing it," that is the definition of an under-scoped agent.

Scope is the prerequisite for autonomy. Without clear boundaries, giving an agent more independence is giving it more rope, and the question is not whether it will cause a problem but when. The teams that build reliable agentic systems are the ones that spend as much time defining what the agent cannot do as they spend building what it can do. That discipline feels conservative. In practice, it is what makes ambitious agentic capabilities possible, because it makes them safe enough to deploy with confidence.

This chapter addressed the structural question: what boundaries does the agent operate within? The next chapter addresses the operational question: where do humans belong in the workflow, and how do you design the handoffs between agent action and human oversight? Chapter 8, Human in the Loop, is the companion to this chapter, and together they form the complete argument for how autonomous systems should be governed.

Human in the Loop

Part IV: Agents

Full automation is not the finish line. It is often not even the right goal. The most reliable AI systems know where humans belong in the workflow and design those handoffs intentionally.

Designing Human Checkpoints

There is a narrative in AI that positions human involvement as a temporary limitation. The system needs a human in the loop now, but the goal is to remove them eventually. Full autonomy is the endgame. Human oversight is a training wheel.

This narrative is wrong for most production systems, and following it leads to architectures that treat human involvement as a cost to minimize rather than a capability to design for.

Humans bring things to a workflow that AI systems do not have and will not have for the foreseeable future: domain judgment that accounts for context the system cannot see, ethical reasoning about edge cases that were not anticipated, accountability that matters to stakeholders and regulators, and the ability to recognize when something looks technically correct but is substantively wrong. These are not limitations of current models that will be resolved with the next release. They are structural properties of the role humans play in consequential decision-making.

A human checkpoint is a designed moment in a workflow where a human reviews, approves, modifies, or overrides an agent's action before it takes effect. The key word is "designed." A checkpoint that is thrown in as an afterthought, a generic "are you sure?" dialog that users learn to click through without reading, is not a checkpoint. It is decoration. A real checkpoint is a point in the workflow where the system presents the human with the information they need to make a judgment, in a format that supports fast and accurate decision-making, at a moment when their judgment actually matters.

Designing effective checkpoints starts with identifying which actions in the workflow benefit from human judgment. Not every action does. An agent that tags a support ticket with a category does not need a human to approve the tag. The cost of a wrong tag is low, and the correction is easy. An agent that drafts a response to a customer complaint and is about to send it does benefit from human review, because the cost of a bad response is reputational, and the nuances of tone and context are difficult for the model to get right consistently.

The decision of where to place checkpoints should be driven by the trust levels from Chapter 7. Level 1 and Level 2 actions, read-only and reversible, generally do not need checkpoints. Level 3 actions, consequential but with human confirmation, are where checkpoints live. Level 4 actions, autonomous and consequential, are where checkpoints have been deliberately removed based on demonstrated performance. The progression from Level 3 to Level 4 is the progression from "human reviews every action" to "human reviews exceptions only." That progression should be evidence-based, not assumption-based.

A common mistake is placing checkpoints at the wrong granularity. If the agent performs a five-step workflow and the checkpoint is at the end, the human is reviewing the final output without seeing the intermediate reasoning. If any intermediate step was flawed, the final output might look plausible but be based on an incorrect premise. The human approves it because the surface looks fine. A better design places the checkpoint at the step where the most consequential judgment occurs. In a workflow where the agent classifies a request, researches the answer, drafts a response, and sends it, the checkpoint should probably be after the draft, where the human can evaluate the response in context. Placing it after the classification would catch routing errors but not drafting errors. Placing it after sending defeats the purpose entirely.

Let me illustrate with a system I worked on. An agent was responsible for generating quarterly business review summaries from a set of dashboards and data sources. The original design had a single checkpoint at the end: a human reviewed the finished summary before it was distributed to stakeholders. In practice, the human reviewer was spending twenty minutes per summary, not because the summaries were bad, but because they could not tell whether the numbers were correct without going back to the source dashboards. The checkpoint was at the wrong point.

The redesign added an earlier checkpoint: after the data extraction step, the agent presented a structured data table showing every number it had pulled and its source. The human spent two minutes verifying the numbers. Once verified, the summary generation step could proceed with confidence that its inputs were correct, and the final review shrank to five minutes of checking tone and narrative rather than re-verifying every number. Total review time dropped from twenty minutes to seven, and review quality actually improved because the human was doing focused verification at the right level of granularity at each step.

The lesson is that checkpoint placement is a design decision with significant impact on both effectiveness and efficiency. A checkpoint at the wrong point in the workflow is worse than no checkpoint at all, because it creates a false sense of oversight without providing real protection. The right placement requires understanding the workflow well enough to know where human judgment adds the most value and where errors are most consequential.

Interrupt Patterns

An interrupt is a point where the agent pauses its workflow and hands control to a human. Not every checkpoint is an interrupt. A checkpoint can be asynchronous: the agent queues its action for human review and moves on to other work. An interrupt is synchronous: the agent stops and waits for human input before proceeding.

The choice between synchronous and asynchronous depends on the workflow and the consequences of proceeding without approval.

Synchronous interrupts are appropriate when the action is irreversible or when the cost of proceeding incorrectly is high enough to justify blocking the workflow. An agent about to execute a financial transaction should stop and wait. An agent about to delete data should stop and wait. An agent about to send an external communication to a high-value client should stop and wait. The latency cost of waiting for human input is real, but it is smaller than the cost of the action going wrong.

Asynchronous checkpoints are appropriate when the action is reversible or when the workflow can continue with provisional results that the human will review later. An agent that generates reports and queues them for human review before distribution is using an asynchronous checkpoint. The agent is not blocked. The reports sit in a review queue. The human reviews them when they have time. If the reports are time-sensitive, the queue has a deadline that triggers an alert if the review is not completed. This pattern keeps the agent productive while maintaining human oversight.

Exception-based interrupts are a hybrid pattern where the agent operates autonomously unless it encounters a situation that exceeds its confidence threshold or falls outside its defined scope. The agent processes routine cases without interruption but flags exceptions for human attention. This is the pattern that most mature agentic systems converge on, because it concentrates human attention where it has the most value: on the cases the agent is least equipped to handle.

The design of the interrupt itself matters as much as the decision to interrupt. When the agent pauses and presents a decision to a human, the presentation should be optimized for fast, accurate judgment. That means showing the proposed action clearly, providing the context that led to the action, highlighting any factors the human should pay special attention to, and making it easy to approve, modify, or reject. A confirmation dialog that says "Send email? Yes / No" is a bad interrupt. A confirmation dialog that shows the draft email, the customer context, the classification that led to this draft, the confidence score, and any flags for unusual content is a good interrupt. The quality of the interrupt determines the quality of the human judgment, which determines whether the checkpoint actually works.

One antipattern to watch for: interrupt fatigue. If the system interrupts the human too frequently, the human starts approving without reviewing. This is the "alarm fatigue" problem from medicine and aviation applied to AI workflows. The human becomes desensitized because the vast majority of interrupts require no action, and the cognitive cost of carefully reviewing each one exceeds the perceived benefit. The solution is not to remove interrupts. It is to make them rarer and more meaningful by increasing the agent's autonomy on routine cases and only interrupting for genuinely uncertain or high-risk situations. Every interrupt should represent a case where human judgment is likely to change the outcome. If the human approves 99 percent of interrupts without modification, the interrupt threshold is too sensitive and should be recalibrated.

There is a subtler form of interrupt failure that is worth naming: context-switching cost. Every interrupt pulls the human out of whatever they were doing and forces them to load the context of the agent's decision into their working memory. If the human is a customer support manager and the agent interrupts them while they are handling a live customer interaction, the context switch is costly in both time and attention. The design of the interrupt should account for this. Non-urgent interrupts should be batched or queued rather than pushed immediately. Urgent interrupts should include enough context that the human can make the decision quickly without having to investigate. And the system should be aware of the human's current state, if possible, to avoid interrupting at the worst possible moment.

One team I worked with tracked the average decision time for each type of interrupt and used it as a design metric. If a particular interrupt type consistently took the reviewer more than two minutes to resolve, they treated that as a signal that the interrupt interface was not providing enough context. They would redesign the interrupt to include the missing information, then measure whether decision time improved. Over three months, they reduced the average interrupt resolution time from 90 seconds to 25 seconds, which meant the same human reviewer could handle three times as many interrupts with higher accuracy. The metric was simple, but it created a continuous improvement loop for the human-in-the-loop experience.

Confidence-Gated Approval

Chapter 2 introduced confidence thresholds as a design tool for probabilistic systems. In agentic workflows, confidence thresholds become the gate that determines whether an action proceeds automatically or requires human approval. This is confidence-gated approval, and it is the mechanism that connects the trust level framework from Chapter 7 with the checkpoint design in this chapter.

The pattern works as follows. For each action the agent can take, you define a confidence threshold. When the agent prepares to take the action, it generates a confidence score. If the score is above the threshold, the action proceeds automatically at whatever trust level it has been granted. If the score is below the threshold, the action is routed to a human for review, regardless of its trust level. This creates a dynamic system where the agent's autonomy adjusts based on its confidence in each specific decision rather than being fixed globally.

The confidence score can be derived from multiple sources, as discussed in Chapter 2: the model's self-reported confidence, consistency checks from multiple runs, structural validation of the output, or secondary model evaluation. For agentic actions, there is an additional source worth incorporating: historical accuracy at similar confidence levels. If you have data showing that the agent's actions are correct 98 percent of the time when its confidence score is above 0.85, but only 75 percent of the time when the score is between 0.7 and 0.85, you can set the approval threshold at 0.85 with empirical backing. Actions above 0.85 proceed automatically. Actions between 0.7 and 0.85 go to human review. Actions below 0.7 are rejected or routed to a fallback path.

Confidence gating solves the interrupt fatigue problem described in the previous section. Instead of interrupting the human on every consequential action, you interrupt only on actions where the agent's confidence is low enough that human judgment is likely to matter. High-confidence actions proceed automatically, keeping the workflow fast. Low-confidence actions get human review, keeping the workflow safe. The threshold is the tuning knob, and you adjust it based on the data: if too many actions are being routed to human review and the human is approving most of them without changes, the threshold is too conservative and should be raised. If actions are proceeding automatically but too many of them turn out to be wrong, the threshold is too permissive and should be lowered.

The organizational implication of confidence-gated approval is that the human's role shifts from reviewing everything to reviewing exceptions. This is a different skill and a different workflow than blanket approval. The human needs to be prepared for the fact that the cases they see are the hard ones, the ones where the agent was uncertain, where the input was ambiguous, or where the situation was unusual. This changes the design of the review interface: it should emphasize the factors that made the agent uncertain, not just present the proposed action. The human is not rubber-stamping routine decisions. They are applying judgment to the cases that most need it. Designing the experience to reflect that, highlighting uncertainty and providing context for why the human is being asked, is what makes the checkpoint genuinely useful rather than performative.

There is a feedback loop built into confidence-gated approval that is worth calling out explicitly. Every human review produces data: was the action approved, modified, or rejected? What was the confidence score? What was the actual outcome? This data feeds back into the confidence calibration. If the human approves most actions at a confidence score of 0.80, the system can learn that 0.80 is reliable enough for automatic processing. If the human frequently modifies actions even at a confidence score of 0.90, the threshold needs to be higher, or the confidence scoring mechanism itself needs recalibration. Over time, this feedback loop tightens the alignment between the agent's confidence estimates and the actual probability of a good outcome, which means the human's time is spent more efficiently and the agent's autonomy is more precisely calibrated.

This feedback loop also provides a natural mechanism for the progressive expansion plan described in Chapter 7. As the confidence calibration improves and the data shows that high-confidence actions are reliably correct, the team has the evidence to raise trust levels for specific actions. The expansion is not based on intuition or organizational pressure. It is based on measured performance over a defined period, which is exactly the kind of evidence-based decision-making that builds durable trust in the system.

Reducing Friction in Oversight

The tension in every human-in-the-loop system is between oversight quality and workflow speed. Too much oversight and the system is slow, expensive, and frustrating. Too little and the system is fast but unreliable. The goal is not to pick a side. It is to reduce the friction of oversight so that high-quality human judgment does not come at an unacceptable cost to workflow speed.

Friction reduction starts with the information presented at each checkpoint. The fastest human reviews are the ones where the human has everything they need to make a decision in a single view, without clicking through tabs, searching for context, or mentally reconstructing the agent's reasoning. This means the checkpoint interface should include: the proposed action, the key context that informed it, the agent's confidence score, any flags or anomalies, and clear approve/modify/reject controls. If the human has to leave the checkpoint interface to gather information before making a decision, the interface is incomplete.

Batching is a powerful friction reduction technique for workflows with high volume. Instead of presenting each action individually, the system batches similar actions together and presents them as a group. A human reviewing ten tagged support tickets can process them faster as a batch, scanning for outliers, than reviewing each one individually. Batching works best when the actions are similar enough that reviewing them together provides context that individual reviews would lack. If the batch is heterogeneous, it does not save time and may reduce quality.

Pre-populated modifications reduce friction for the common case where the human wants to make a small change rather than accept or reject outright. If the agent drafted an email and the human wants to adjust one sentence, the interface should support inline editing of the draft rather than requiring the human to reject the action and manually rewrite the entire email. The closer the interface is to "tweak and approve" rather than "reject and redo," the faster the oversight cycle and the more likely the human is to actually make the corrections rather than approving despite seeing an issue.

There is also a design pattern I call progressive disclosure of oversight. For routine actions where the agent's confidence is high, the checkpoint can be minimal: a notification that the action was taken, with an option to review or undo. For unusual actions where the agent's confidence is lower, the checkpoint can be more detailed: the full action with context and an explicit approval step. For exceptional actions where the agent flagged significant uncertainty, the checkpoint can be comprehensive: a detailed explanation of the reasoning, the alternative actions considered, and a structured review form. This graduated approach matches the level of human attention to the level of risk, which is both more efficient and more effective than applying the same review depth to every action regardless of confidence.

A final point on friction: the human reviewer's experience is a product design problem, not just an engineering problem. If the review interface is clunky, slow, or confusing, the reviewer will either rush through it or avoid it. Both outcomes defeat the purpose of having a human in the loop. Invest in the review experience the same way you invest in the user experience. The reviewer is a user of your system, and their effectiveness is a direct function of how well the interface supports their judgment. The best review interfaces I have seen treat the reviewer's time as precious and their judgment as the product: they surface exactly the right information, at the right level of detail, in a format that enables a confident decision in seconds rather than minutes.

Audit Trails and Accountability

Every action an agent takes should be logged with enough detail to reconstruct, after the fact, what happened, why it happened, and who was responsible for authorizing it. This is not optional. It is the minimum standard for accountability in systems that make consequential decisions.

An audit log for an agentic action should include: the action that was taken, the timestamp, the input that triggered it, the agent's reasoning or the intermediate outputs that led to the decision, the confidence score, the trust level, whether a human was in the loop, and if so, who approved it and what (if anything) they modified. This is more detail than most teams log initially, and the common objection is that it is expensive to store and tedious to implement. Both of those objections are valid and both are outweighed by the value the logs provide when something goes wrong.

Audit logs serve three distinct purposes, and understanding all three is important for designing them well.

Incident investigation. When an agent takes an incorrect action, the audit log is how you determine what happened. Without it, you are guessing. With it, you can trace the exact chain of events: what input the agent received, how it interpreted the input, which tools it called, what outputs it generated at each step, what confidence score it assigned, and whether a human reviewed and approved the action. This trace tells you whether the failure was in the agent's reasoning, in the context it was given, in the tools it used, or in the human review that missed the problem. Each of these has a different fix, and without the trace, you cannot tell which one applies.

Continuous improvement. Audit logs are a source of evaluation data. Every logged action is a potential test case for your eval suite. Actions that were approved by humans and resulted in good outcomes are positive examples. Actions that were modified by humans reveal where the agent's judgment diverges from human judgment. Actions that caused problems are negative examples. Over time, the audit log becomes a dataset that you can use to improve the agent's prompts, its confidence calibration, and its scope definition. Teams that mine their audit logs systematically improve faster than teams that treat the logs as a compliance artifact.

Compliance and trust. In regulated industries, audit trails are a legal requirement. But even outside of regulated industries, audit trails build organizational trust in the agentic system. When stakeholders can see what the agent did and why, they are more comfortable granting it additional autonomy. When they cannot, every expansion of the agent's scope feels like a leap of faith. The audit trail is the evidence base for the progressive expansion plan from Chapter 7. It is how you demonstrate to yourself and to others that the agent is operating within its designed parameters and producing the expected results.

A common shortcoming in audit trail design is logging the action but not the context. Knowing that the agent sent an email to a customer at 3:47 PM is not useful for investigation. Knowing that the agent sent the email because the customer filed a complaint classified as high-priority, that the agent drafted the email using a specific template, that the agent's confidence score was 0.91, and that the email was approved by a human reviewer who modified the closing paragraph, that is useful. The log should tell the story of the decision, not just record the outcome.

One implementation note: separate the audit log from the application log. Application logs are for debugging the system. Audit logs are for understanding the agent's decisions. They have different retention requirements, different access control needs, and different consumers. The application log can be rotated and archived aggressively. The audit log should be retained for as long as the decisions it records could be questioned, which in some contexts is years. Mixing the two leads to audit data being lost in log rotation or application debug data being retained longer than necessary.

Engineering Heuristics

Heuristic 1: Design human checkpoints before optimizing them away.

Start with more human oversight than you think you need. Put a checkpoint on every consequential action. Then, as you gather data on the agent's accuracy and the human's review patterns, selectively remove checkpoints where the data shows they are not changing outcomes. This is the opposite of the common approach, which is to launch with minimal oversight and add checkpoints after something goes wrong. Starting with checkpoints and removing them is safe. Starting without checkpoints and adding them is reactive. The data from the initial checkpoints also gives you the baseline you need to set confidence thresholds for confidence-gated approval.

Heuristic 2: An approval flow nobody uses is not oversight, it is theater.

If you have an approval step and the human approves 100 percent of actions without modification, you do not have oversight. You have a speed bump that the human has learned to click through. This happens when the approval flow is too frequent, when it does not provide enough context for meaningful review, or when the human has no practical way to modify or reject without disrupting the workflow. If your approval rates are above 98 percent with zero modifications, either the agent is remarkably good and the checkpoint can be removed, or the checkpoint is poorly designed and the human is rubber-stamping. Investigate which one it is. The data will tell you.

Heuristic 3: Log every autonomous action with enough context to reconstruct intent.

For every action the agent takes, whether or not a human was in the loop, the log should answer: what did the agent do, what information did it base the decision on, how confident was it, and what was the outcome? This is the minimum for accountability. If you cannot reconstruct why the agent took a specific action from the log alone, the log is incomplete. Build this logging from the start, not after the first incident. The cost of comprehensive logging is small. The cost of investigating an incident without it is large. And the value of the logs as training data for improving the agent is a bonus that compounds over time.

Chapters 7 and 8 form the agents pair. Chapter 7 defined the boundaries: what the agent can do, what tools it has access to, what trust levels govern its actions. This chapter defined the human layer: where humans belong in the workflow, how to design the handoffs, and how to maintain accountability for the agent's actions. Together they argue that autonomy is not a binary switch but a spectrum, calibrated to risk, earned through demonstrated reliability, and always accountable through audit trails.

With Parts I through IV complete, the book has covered how to think about AI systems, how to feed them, how to instruct them, and how to govern them when they act. What remains is how to know whether any of this is working. Part V turns to measurement and resilience, starting with Chapter 9: Eval-First Development.

Eval-First Development

Part V: Eval

Testing AI systems requires a different mindset than testing traditional software. You cannot write unit tests for probabilistic outputs and expect them to hold. Define what good looks like before you build, then construct the measurement infrastructure alongside the system itself.

What Makes a Good Eval

The word "eval" in AI engineering covers a lot of ground. It can mean anything from a quick eyeball test on a few examples to a rigorous, automated scoring pipeline running against thousands of test cases. The gap between these two ends of the spectrum is where most teams run into trouble. They know they should be evaluating their AI features. They are not sure what a good evaluation actually looks like. So they do something minimal, convince themselves it is enough, and move on.

The cost of this approach becomes clear over time. Without a real eval, every change to the system is a coin flip. Did the new prompt improve quality? You think so, based on a few examples you tried. Did the context pipeline change degrade output? You do not know, because you did not measure before and after. Is the system better today than it was a month ago? No idea. The team is flying blind, making changes based on intuition, and the system's quality is whatever it happens to be rather than what it was engineered to be.

Eval-first development inverts this. You define what good looks like before you build. You construct the measurement infrastructure alongside the system. And you use the measurements to drive every subsequent decision. It is the same philosophy as test-driven development in traditional software, adapted for the reality that AI outputs are probabilistic and quality is a spectrum rather than a binary.

A good eval has five properties. Understanding these upfront is what separates teams that iterate effectively from teams that wander.

It measures what matters. This sounds obvious but it is routinely violated. A team building a summarization feature measures whether the summary is a valid string of English text. It always is. The metric is green. The feature ships. Users complain that the summaries miss key points and sometimes include fabricated details. The eval measured the wrong thing. It measured whether the output was well-formed, not whether the output was useful. A good eval measures the properties that determine whether users will be satisfied and whether the system is achieving its intended purpose. For a summarization feature, that means measuring coverage of key points, factual accuracy against the source, appropriate length, and absence of hallucinated content. Each of these is a distinct dimension that should be scored independently.

It uses representative inputs. An eval that runs against ten carefully selected examples will give you a misleadingly optimistic picture. Those examples were probably chosen because they are clean, typical, and easy for the system to handle. A good eval runs against inputs that represent the actual distribution of what the system will encounter in production, including the messy, ambiguous, and edge-case inputs that are where most failures occur. The eval dataset should include inputs that are easy, inputs that are hard, inputs that are ambiguous, and inputs that are outside the expected scope. The proportions should roughly match what the system will actually see.

It produces a score, not a pass/fail. Binary pass/fail evaluations are useful for structural checks but insufficient for quality assessment. A good eval produces a numerical score on a defined scale, and that score can be tracked over time, compared across prompt versions, and decomposed into component dimensions. A score of 4.2 out of 5 on factual accuracy is actionable information. "Pass" is not. Scores let you see trends: is quality improving, stable, or degrading? Scores let you set thresholds: we ship when quality is above 4.0 and investigate when it drops below 3.8. Scores let you compare: prompt version A scored 4.1 and version B scored 4.4. Binary pass/fail hides all of this information.

It is reproducible. Running the eval twice on the same system should produce similar results. Not identical, because the system is probabilistic, but similar enough that the score is stable and meaningful. If your eval produces a score of 3.8 on one run and 4.5 on the next, the eval is too noisy to be useful. Reproducibility requires a large enough dataset, consistent scoring criteria, and enough runs to average out the variance. A common approach is to run the eval three to five times and report the mean and standard deviation. If the standard deviation is large relative to the differences you are trying to detect, you need a larger dataset or a more stable scoring method.

It is fast enough to use. An eval that takes three days to run will not be used frequently. An eval that takes thirty minutes will be used on every prompt change. Speed affects how tightly the eval integrates into your development workflow. The ideal is an eval that runs automatically as part of your deployment pipeline, blocking changes that degrade quality. If the full eval is too slow for that, build a smaller fast eval that catches obvious regressions and run the full eval on a schedule, perhaps nightly or weekly. The key is that the eval must be practical enough that the team actually uses it, rather than running it once and then forgetting about it.

Golden Datasets

A golden dataset is a curated collection of input-output pairs where the expected output represents the best possible answer. It is the ground truth that your eval scores against. The quality of your golden dataset determines the quality of your eval, which determines the quality of your iteration cycle. There is no shortcut here. A weak golden dataset produces misleading eval scores, which lead to misguided optimization, which produces a worse system than the one you started with.

Building a golden dataset is labor-intensive, which is why teams cut corners on it. The most common shortcut is to use the model's own outputs as the golden data: run the system on a set of inputs, eyeball the outputs, mark the ones that look good, and call that the golden dataset. This is circular. You are evaluating the model against its own output, which means you are measuring self-consistency, not quality. The model might be consistently wrong in ways that look plausible, and the golden dataset will not catch it.

I watched this play out with a team building an AI feature that generated product descriptions for an e-commerce platform. They created their golden dataset by running the model on 100 products and selecting the descriptions that looked good. Their eval scores were consistently high. Then a domain expert, a merchandising manager with fifteen years of experience, reviewed the golden dataset and found that nearly a third of the descriptions contained subtle inaccuracies: wrong material descriptions, misleading sizing language, and feature claims that were technically true for a different product in the same line but not for the specific product being described. The model's descriptions were fluent and convincing. They were also wrong in ways that the model's own self-assessment could not detect. The golden dataset needed to be rebuilt by people who knew the products, not by the model that was getting them wrong.

Good golden datasets come from domain experts. If your system summarizes legal contracts, the golden summaries should be written by paralegals or attorneys who know what a good contract summary looks like. If your system classifies support tickets, the golden classifications should come from experienced support agents who understand the category taxonomy and the edge cases. The expertise of the person creating the golden data directly determines its value as a benchmark.

Golden datasets should cover the full range of inputs the system will encounter, not just the typical ones. Specifically, a well-designed golden dataset includes:

Typical cases that represent the bread and butter of the system's workload. These should constitute the majority of the dataset, because they are what the system handles most often and where baseline quality matters most.

Edge cases that test the system's behavior on unusual, ambiguous, or boundary inputs. These are where most quality failures occur in production, and they are systematically underrepresented in datasets that are built casually.

Adversarial cases that test the system's robustness against inputs designed to cause failures: prompt injection attempts, nonsensical inputs, inputs in the wrong format, inputs that are extremely long or extremely short.

Known failure cases from production. When a user reports a problem or a human reviewer corrects an agent's output, that input-correction pair should be added to the golden dataset. These are the most valuable additions because they represent real failures that the system needs to handle better. Over time, this creates a dataset that is specifically tuned to the system's actual weaknesses.

The golden dataset is a living artifact. It should grow over time as new cases are discovered and new edge cases emerge. It should be version-controlled, so you can track how the dataset has changed and correlate those changes with eval score movements. And it should be reviewed periodically by domain experts to ensure the golden outputs are still correct and still represent the current standard of quality. A golden dataset that was created a year ago and never updated is a golden dataset that is evaluating against an outdated standard.

Size matters, but less than quality. A golden dataset of 200 carefully curated, expert-labeled examples is more valuable than a dataset of 2,000 auto-generated examples with spotty labels. Start small and high-quality. Expand deliberately, adding cases that cover gaps in the existing dataset rather than adding volume for its own sake. A practical starting point for most systems is 50 to 100 examples that cover the core use cases and the most important edge cases. You can expand from there as the system matures and as production data reveals new failure modes to cover.

LLM-as-Judge Patterns

Human evaluation is the gold standard for assessing AI output quality, but it does not scale. Having a domain expert score every output in a 200-case eval suite takes hours. Doing it on every prompt change is impractical. This is where LLM-as-judge comes in: using a language model to evaluate the outputs of another language model.

The pattern is straightforward. You take the system's output, combine it with the input and the golden reference (if available), and ask a judge model to score the output on defined criteria. The judge model returns a score and often a justification. The scores are aggregated across the eval dataset to produce an overall quality metric.

LLM-as-judge has become widely used because it offers a middle ground between expensive human evaluation and cheap-but-shallow automated checks. A well-designed LLM judge can approximate human judgment on many quality dimensions: factual accuracy, completeness, tone, format compliance, relevance. It is not perfect, and it should not replace human evaluation entirely, but it makes frequent, detailed evaluation practical in a way that purely human evaluation does not.

Designing a good judge prompt requires the same discipline as designing any other prompt (see Chapters 5 and 6). The judge needs a clear rubric: what does a score of 1 mean versus a score of 5? It needs examples of outputs at different quality levels. It needs explicit instructions about what to prioritize and what to ignore. A vague judge prompt produces vague, inconsistent scores that are not useful for decision-making.

Rubric design is where most LLM-as-judge implementations succeed or fail. A rubric that says "rate this output from 1 to 5 on quality" is too vague to produce consistent scores. A rubric that says "rate factual accuracy from 1 to 5, where 1 means multiple factual errors that contradict the source, 2 means one significant factual error, 3 means factually accurate but missing important context, 4 means factually accurate with relevant context, and 5 means factually accurate, complete, and properly contextualized" gives the judge a clear standard at each score level. The difference in scoring consistency is dramatic. Invest the time to define each level explicitly, with examples, for every dimension you are evaluating. This upfront work pays off on every subsequent eval run.

There are several patterns for LLM-as-judge evaluation that serve different purposes:

Reference-based scoring. The judge compares the system's output to the golden reference and scores how well the output matches. This works well for tasks with objectively correct answers, like fact extraction or classification. The judge has a clear standard to compare against.

Reference-free scoring. The judge evaluates the system's output on its own merits, without a golden reference. This is necessary for open-ended tasks like creative writing or conversational responses where there is no single correct answer. The judge scores based on general quality criteria: is it coherent, relevant, well-structured, free of errors?

Pairwise comparison. The judge compares two outputs side by side and determines which one is better. This is particularly useful for A/B testing prompt versions: show the judge the output from prompt A and prompt B for the same input, and ask which is higher quality. Pairwise comparison is often more reliable than absolute scoring, because relative judgments are easier for both humans and models than absolute ones.

A critical practice: validate your judge. Before relying on LLM-as-judge scores for decision-making, run a calibration study. Have both the judge model and human evaluators score the same set of outputs. Compare the scores. If they correlate well, the judge is a reliable proxy for human judgment on those criteria. If they diverge significantly, the judge prompt needs refinement, or the quality dimension being measured may be one that models cannot reliably assess. Do not assume the judge is accurate. Verify it. A miscalibrated judge is worse than no judge, because it gives you confidence in decisions that the data does not actually support.

One important caveat: using the same model to generate output and to judge that output introduces bias. The model tends to rate its own output style more favorably than other styles. When possible, use a different model as the judge than the one generating the output. If that is not practical, at least be aware of the bias and calibrate your scores against periodic human evaluations.

Regression Testing for AI

In traditional software, a regression is a bug introduced by a change: something that used to work now does not. In AI systems, regressions happen in all the usual ways plus several new ones. A prompt change can degrade quality. A context pipeline change can alter what the model sees. A model update from the provider can shift behavior. A change in the input distribution can expose weaknesses that did not exist in the previous distribution. And all of these can happen simultaneously, making diagnosis significantly harder.

Regression testing for AI means running your eval suite regularly and comparing the results to a known baseline. The baseline is the eval score from a known-good state of the system: the version that is currently in production, or the last version that passed a full quality review. Every change, whether to the prompt, the context pipeline, the model version, or the system configuration, should be evaluated against this baseline before deployment.

The challenge is that AI eval scores have natural variance. Running the same eval twice might produce scores of 4.21 and 4.18. That is not a regression. That is noise. A drop from 4.21 to 4.05 might be a regression, or it might be noise from a different sample of probabilistic outputs. Distinguishing real regressions from noise requires statistical discipline: enough eval runs to establish confidence intervals, defined thresholds for what constitutes a significant change, and awareness that small-looking differences can be meaningful if they are consistent across multiple runs.

A practical regression testing workflow looks like this. Before deploying any change, run the eval suite three times against the current version (baseline) and three times against the proposed change. Compare the means. If the proposed change scores within one standard deviation of the baseline on all quality dimensions, it is likely safe to deploy. If it scores significantly lower on any dimension, investigate before deploying. If it scores significantly higher, celebrate, but still investigate to understand why, because unexpected improvements can indicate the eval is measuring something different rather than the system actually being better.

There is a category of regression that is particularly insidious in AI systems: the silent model regression. This happens when the model provider updates the model and the behavior changes without any notification. Your code has not changed. Your prompts have not changed. Your context pipeline has not changed. But the outputs are different because the model underneath is different. The only way to catch this is to run your eval suite regularly even when you have made no changes. A weekly eval run that compares against the baseline catches model-side regressions that would otherwise go unnoticed until a user reports a problem, which could be days or weeks later.

This is one of the strongest arguments for the eval-first approach. If you build the eval suite before or alongside the system, you have a regression detection capability from day one. If you build the eval suite later, you spend the intervening period blind to regressions. And the longer you go without eval coverage, the more regressions accumulate undetected, and the harder it becomes to establish a clean baseline when you finally do build the suite.

There is an organizational dimension to regression testing that is worth addressing. In many teams, regression testing is treated as a gate before release: run the tests, check the results, ship or fix. In AI systems, regression testing also needs to be a continuous monitoring practice. The weekly eval run is not gating a release. It is checking whether the system's quality is holding steady in the absence of any changes on your side. This is a different cadence and a different mindset than release-gated testing. Both are necessary. Release-gated testing catches regressions you introduced. Continuous testing catches regressions that arrived from outside, through model updates, data distribution shifts, or retrieval quality degradation.

Eval-Driven Iteration Loops

The ultimate purpose of an eval suite is not to measure quality. It is to improve quality. The eval is the feedback mechanism that drives the iteration cycle. Without it, iteration is guesswork: you change something, try a few examples, and decide whether it feels better. With it, iteration is engineering: you change something, run the eval, and know whether it is better, by how much, and on which dimensions.

An eval-driven iteration loop has four steps that repeat:

Step one: identify the weakest dimension. Run the eval and look at the scores by dimension. Which quality dimension has the lowest score? Where is the system underperforming relative to the target? This is where your next improvement effort should focus. Working on the weakest dimension produces the largest marginal improvement, which is a more efficient use of engineering time than polishing a dimension that is already strong.

Step two: diagnose the root cause. Examine the specific eval cases where the system scored poorly on the target dimension. What went wrong? Was it a context issue, where the right information was not in the window? A prompt issue, where the instructions were ambiguous? A model limitation, where the task exceeds the model's current capability? A golden dataset issue, where the expected output is unrealistic? The diagnosis determines the fix. Applying a prompt fix to a context problem wastes time. Diagnosing correctly saves it.

Step three: implement and measure the fix. Make the change and run the eval. Did the target dimension improve? Did any other dimension degrade? A fix that improves factual accuracy but degrades response length or tone is not necessarily a net positive. The eval should be run across all dimensions for every change, not just the dimension you were targeting, because improvements in one area can cause regressions in another.

Step four: update the baseline. If the change is an improvement across the board, update the baseline. The new eval scores become the standard that future changes are compared against. If the change is a mixed result, decide whether the trade-off is acceptable and document the decision. Over time, this creates a clear history of quality evolution: what changed, when, why, and what the impact was.

This loop is the operational core of AI product development. Teams that run it tightly, making changes, measuring impact, and iterating based on data, improve faster and more reliably than teams that rely on intuition and spot-checking. The eval suite is what makes the loop possible. Without it, every step is a guess. With it, every step is a measurement.

One organizational point worth making: the eval-driven loop works best when the eval results are visible to the team, not locked in a dashboard that one person checks occasionally. Post eval scores in the team channel after every run. Celebrate improvements. Investigate declines collectively. When the team sees quality as a number that they are collectively responsible for, the quality culture shifts from "someone should test this" to "we know exactly where we stand and what to improve next." That shift is more valuable than any individual prompt optimization.

Engineering Heuristics

Heuristic 1: Define your success criteria before writing your first prompt.

This is the eval-first principle in its most distilled form. Before you write a prompt, answer the questions: what does a good output look like? What does an acceptable output look like? What does an unacceptable output look like? How will I score the difference between these categories? Write the scoring rubric. Create the first ten golden dataset entries. Set a target score. Then write the prompt. This order is counterintuitive for engineers who want to build first and measure later, but it is the order that produces the best results, because it forces you to be precise about what you are building before you build it. Vague goals produce vague systems. Specific eval criteria produce specific, measurable improvement.

Heuristic 2: An eval suite is a product artifact, not a testing afterthought.

The eval suite should be maintained with the same rigor as the product code. It should live in version control. Changes to it should be reviewed. It should have an owner. It should be run regularly and the results should be tracked over time. When the product changes, the eval should be updated to reflect the new requirements. When a new failure mode is discovered, it should be added to the eval. The eval suite is not overhead. It is the tool that makes reliable iteration possible. Teams that treat it as an afterthought iterate slowly and unreliably. Teams that invest in it iterate fast with confidence.

Heuristic 3: Curate your golden dataset with the same care as your training data.

The golden dataset is the standard your system is measured against. If the standard is low quality, incorrect, or unrepresentative, your eval will reward the wrong behaviors and penalize the right ones. Invest in expert-labeled golden data. Review it periodically. Update it as the domain evolves. Add production failure cases as they are discovered. Remove examples that no longer represent current quality standards. A golden dataset is not a one-time deliverable. It is a living artifact that evolves with the system, and its quality directly determines how well your eval-driven iteration loop works.

Eval-first development is the discipline that connects every other principle in this book to measurable outcomes. Context architecture from Part II improves output quality, but you only know by how much if you measure it. Prompt design from Part III makes the system more reliable, but you only know which prompt version is best if you compare eval scores. Agent scoping from Part IV keeps the system safe, but you only know the agent is performing within its scope if you evaluate it continuously.

This chapter covered what to measure and how to measure it. The next chapter covers what to do when the measurements show a failure: graceful degradation. Because in a probabilistic system, failures are not anomalies to eliminate. They are a structural feature to design around. Chapter 10 addresses that design challenge directly.

Graceful Degradation

Part V: Eval

AI systems fail in ways that traditional software does not. A model can hallucinate, drift, time out, or return low-confidence output at any moment. Fallback is a feature, not an afterthought.

Failure Taxonomy for AI

Chapter 2 introduced the concept that AI systems fail differently from traditional software. This chapter makes that concept operational. Before you can design graceful degradation, you need to understand the specific ways your system can fail, because each failure type requires a different response.

Chapter 2 cataloged five failure modes: hallucination, drift, boundary confusion, format violation, and refusal. Those categories describe what goes wrong with the model's output. But in production, failures also occur at every other layer of the system. A complete failure taxonomy for an AI-driven application includes failures at the model layer, the infrastructure layer, and the integration layer.

Model-layer failures are problems with the quality of the model's output. Hallucination, where the model generates plausible but false information. Drift, where model behavior changes over time without any code change on your side. Boundary confusion, where the model handles ambiguous inputs inconsistently. Refusal, where the model declines to perform a legitimate task. And a category that deserves mention here: degraded reasoning, where the model produces output that is technically responsive but shows shallow or flawed reasoning, particularly on complex multi-step tasks. These are the hardest failures to detect because the output looks normal. Only careful evaluation reveals that the quality has dropped.

Infrastructure-layer failures are problems with the systems that the model depends on. API timeouts, where the model provider takes too long to respond or does not respond at all. Rate limiting, where your request volume exceeds the provider's limits. Service outages, where the model API is temporarily unavailable. Context pipeline failures, where the retrieval system fails to return results, or returns corrupted results. These are more familiar to engineers because they resemble traditional infrastructure failures, but they require AI-specific handling because the system cannot simply retry and expect the same result.

Integration-layer failures are problems at the boundary between the AI system and the rest of your application. Output parsing failures, where the model's response does not conform to the expected format and the downstream code cannot process it. Tool execution failures in agentic systems, where the model requests an action that the tool cannot perform. Context assembly failures, where the context pipeline produces a malformed or incomplete context window. These failures are often the easiest to detect and the easiest to handle, because they occur at well-defined interfaces where validation logic can be placed.

The value of a taxonomy is that it turns a vague concern, "the AI might fail," into a specific set of scenarios, each with its own detection strategy and response plan. A team that has thought through the taxonomy can answer the question: "what happens when X fails?" for every X. A team that has not thought through the taxonomy discovers the answer in production, under pressure, when the failure is already affecting users.

Detection strategies vary by failure type, and this variation is worth understanding. Infrastructure-layer failures are the easiest to detect: a timeout is a timeout, a 500 error is a 500 error, and standard monitoring tools catch them immediately. Integration-layer failures are also relatively easy to detect: output validation catches format violations, and schema checks catch missing fields. Model-layer failures are the hardest to detect, because the output often looks structurally correct but is semantically wrong. Detecting hallucination in real time requires either confidence scoring, secondary model evaluation, or fact-checking against a knowledge base. Detecting drift requires comparing current output quality against a historical baseline. These are the failures that justify the investment in the eval infrastructure from Chapter 9 and the confidence scoring described later in this chapter.

A practical exercise: for each AI feature in your
system, walk through the failure taxonomy and
document the detection strategy and the response for
each failure type. You do not need to implement all of
them at once. But documenting them forces the team
to confront the failure modes explicitly rather than
hoping they will not occur. The documentation
becomes the specification for the fallback
infrastructure you build next.

Fallback Strategies

A fallback is what your system does when the primary
AI-driven path fails. The best fallback strategies share
a common property: they keep the user's experience
intact even though the underlying system is operating
in a degraded state. The user should notice reduced
capability, not a broken experience.

There are several fallback strategies, and the right one
depends on the failure type and the feature.

Retry with modification. For transient failures
like timeouts, rate limits, or format violations, the
simplest fallback is to retry the request. For format
violations, the retry can include additional
instructions: "Your previous response was not valid

JSON. Please respond only with valid JSON matching the following schema." For timeouts, the retry can use a different model or a shorter context to reduce processing time. Retries should be bounded, typically two or three attempts, with a different fallback if retries are exhausted. Unbounded retries waste resources and delay the user experience without addressing the root cause.

Simpler model fallback. When the primary model is unavailable or too slow, fall back to a simpler, faster, or cheaper model. The output quality may be lower, but the feature still works. This requires the model abstraction discussed in Chapter 11, where your system is not hardcoded to a single model. If you have built the abstraction layer, switching to a fallback model is a configuration change. If you have not, it is an emergency engineering project at the worst possible time.

Cached response. For requests that are similar to previous requests, serve a cached response from a previous successful generation. This works well for features where the same or very similar inputs recur frequently, like FAQ-style support queries or standard document templates. The cached response may not be perfect for the specific request, but it is better than no response. Cache strategies for AI systems should be designed with an awareness that even slightly different inputs may require different outputs, so the similarity threshold for cache hits needs to be calibrated carefully.

Rule-based fallback. For specific, well-defined tasks, a rule-based system can serve as a fallback when the AI path fails. If the AI classification system is down, a keyword-based classifier can route support tickets with reduced accuracy but without interruption. If the AI summarization feature fails, a simple extractive summary that pulls the first and last paragraphs can serve as a placeholder. Rule-based fallbacks are not as good as the AI-driven path, but they are deterministic, fast, and always available. They are the floor that the system cannot drop below.

Human escalation. When no automated fallback can handle the situation adequately, route to a human. This is the most expensive fallback but also the most reliable. The system should make the handoff transparent: the user knows they are being connected to a human, the human receives the context of what the AI system was trying to do and where it failed, and the transition is as smooth as possible. Human escalation should be designed as a first-class workflow, not a last resort that dumps the user into a generic support queue with no context.

These strategies are not mutually exclusive. A well-designed degradation path often chains them: try the primary model, retry once with a modified prompt if it fails, fall back to a simpler model if the retry fails, serve a cached response if the simpler model is also unavailable, and escalate to a human if nothing else works. Each step in the chain is a graceful reduction in capability rather than a cliff edge where the feature simply stops working.

The design of the chain matters. Each level of fallback should be clearly defined in terms of what capability is lost and what capability is preserved. The user should always get something useful, even if it is less useful than the primary path would have provided. A summarization feature that falls back from a detailed analytical summary to a simple extractive summary to a "we could not summarize this document, here are

the first three paragraphs" response is degrading
gracefully at each level. A summarization feature that
goes from a detailed summary to a blank page is not
degrading gracefully. It is crashing with extra steps.

The key design principle is that the fallback should be
designed and tested before the feature ships, not after
the first outage. If the fallback path has never been
exercised, you do not know whether it works. It
should be part of your test suite. Run the feature with
the primary model disabled and verify that the
fallback path activates correctly. Run it with the
fallback model disabled and verify that the next level
of degradation works. Inject simulated failures at each
layer and confirm the system responds as designed.
This is the same discipline as disaster recovery testing
for infrastructure, applied to the AI layer.

One team I worked with ran what they called "chaos
Fridays" for their AI system: once a week, they
deliberately disabled one component of the AI
pipeline in their staging environment and verified that
the degradation paths worked correctly. Over the
course of two months, they found and fixed eleven
degradation bugs that would have been invisible

during normal operation. When their model provider had an actual three-hour outage, the system degraded seamlessly and not a single user reported a problem. The fallback paths had been exercised so thoroughly that the outage was a non-event. That is the operational payoff of testing degradation before you need it.

Confidence Scoring in Production

Chapters 2 and 8 introduced confidence scoring as a design tool. In production, confidence scoring becomes the real-time decision layer that determines whether output is served directly, served with caveats, or routed to a fallback path.

The production implementation of confidence scoring has requirements that go beyond the conceptual framework. It needs to be fast, adding minimal latency to each request. It needs to be reliable, because a confidence scorer that is itself unreliable defeats the purpose. And it needs to be calibrated, meaning the confidence scores should correspond to actual accuracy rates, because the routing decisions depend on that correspondence.

In practice, production confidence scoring often uses a combination of lightweight signals rather than a single expensive evaluation. Structural validation: does the output conform to the expected format? Completeness check: does the output include all required fields? Consistency check: does the output align with the input in obvious ways, such as mentioning the correct entity or referencing the right date? Length check: is the output within the expected range? Each of these is cheap to compute and catches a specific class of failure. Together, they form a composite confidence signal that is fast enough for real-time use.

The composite approach has a practical advantage over a single confidence metric: it is diagnosable. When the composite score is low, you can look at the component scores to understand why. If the structural validation passed but the consistency check failed, the output is well-formatted but may contain incorrect information. If the length check failed but everything else passed, the model may have given a truncated response. This diagnostic capability feeds directly into the fallback selection: different component failures may trigger different fallback strategies. A format violation might trigger a retry with format reinforcement. A consistency failure might trigger a human review. A completeness failure might trigger a supplementary generation step.

For higher-stakes features, the lightweight checks can be supplemented with a secondary model evaluation: a fast, focused judge prompt that scores one or two critical quality dimensions. This adds latency but provides a deeper quality signal. The decision of whether to include this step depends on the cost of serving a bad output versus the cost of the additional latency. For a chat feature where users expect sub-second responses, the lightweight checks alone may be sufficient. For a report generation feature where users expect quality and can tolerate a few extra seconds, the secondary evaluation is worth the investment.

Calibration is an ongoing process. The relationship between confidence scores and actual quality can drift over time, especially when the model updates or the input distribution shifts. Periodic calibration studies, where you compare confidence scores against human quality judgments on a sample of production outputs, keep the scoring accurate. If the calibration drifts, the routing thresholds drift with it, and the system either serves more bad outputs (if confidence scores are inflated) or routes too many outputs to fallback paths (if confidence scores are deflated). Neither is desirable. Quarterly calibration checks are a reasonable cadence for most systems.

User Experience During Failure

How the system communicates failure to the user is as important as how it handles failure technically. A system that fails silently, presenting low-quality output as if it were normal, erodes trust faster than a system that fails honestly.

There are three levels of failure communication, and the right one depends on the severity.

Transparent degradation. The system is operating in a reduced mode, and the user is informed. "Results are being generated by a faster model and may be less detailed than usual." "We could not find relevant information for this query. Here is a general response based on available data." Transparent degradation maintains trust because the user understands that the system is doing its best under constraints. They can calibrate their expectations accordingly and decide whether to proceed or wait.

Uncertainty indicators. The system presents its output with a visual or textual indicator of confidence. A color-coded confidence badge. A note that says "this response has lower confidence and may benefit from manual verification." Uncertainty indicators are particularly important in domains where users might act on the output without question: medical, legal, financial, or any context where the cost of acting on incorrect information is high. The indicator does not prevent the user from using the output. It gives them the information to decide how much to trust it.

Honest failure. The system cannot produce a useful response and says so directly. "I was not able to generate a reliable answer to this question. Here is what I found, but please verify independently." Or simply: "I could not complete this request. Would you like to try rephrasing, or should I connect you with a human agent?" Honest failure is always better than a confident wrong answer. Users can work around a system that tells them it does not know. They cannot work around a system that tells them something incorrect with full confidence.

The worst user experience during failure is the invisible one: the system produces output that is wrong, presents it with full confidence, and the user acts on it. This is the scenario that the entire graceful degradation architecture is designed to prevent. Confidence scoring catches most of these cases by identifying low-quality output before it reaches the user. Fallback paths handle the cases where the primary system cannot produce good output. And failure communication ensures that when degraded output does reach the user, they know to treat it with appropriate caution.

A useful design exercise: for each AI feature, define the failure UX at each degradation level. What does the user see when the system is fully healthy? When it is operating on a fallback model? When the retrieval system is degraded? When the AI system is completely unavailable? Each of these states should have a designed experience, not a generic error page. Users are remarkably tolerant of reduced capability when the system communicates honestly about what is happening. They are remarkably intolerant of systems that pretend everything is fine when it is not.

The design of failure UX also affects how quickly users report genuine problems. A system that communicates degradation honestly trains its users to understand the difference between "the system is operating in a reduced mode" and "the system produced a wrong answer." When users see a confidence indicator or a degradation message, they calibrate their expectations and verify important outputs. When they see no indicators, they assume the system is fully functional and treat every output as reliable. That assumption is what makes silent failures so damaging: the user has no reason to question the output, so the error propagates into whatever decision they make next.

Monitoring and Alerting

Graceful degradation keeps the user experience intact when failures occur. Monitoring and alerting keep the engineering team aware of failures so they can be investigated and resolved. Without monitoring, a system can operate in a degraded state for days or weeks without anyone noticing, because the fallback paths are doing their job well enough that no one complains. That is good for users in the short term and terrible for the system in the long term.

AI system monitoring has three layers that correspond to the failure taxonomy.

Infrastructure monitoring tracks the health of the systems the AI depends on: API latency, error rates, rate limit usage, retrieval system response times, and context pipeline throughput. These are standard operational metrics and most teams already have tooling for them. The AI-specific addition is monitoring these metrics in the context of fallback activation: how often is the fallback model being used? How often are retries being triggered? How often is the human escalation path activated? These rates are the pulse of the degradation system. A rising fallback rate means something is wrong upstream.

Quality monitoring tracks the quality of the system's output over time. This is where the eval infrastructure from Chapter 9 becomes an operational tool. Run a lightweight eval on a sample of production outputs continuously, scoring key quality dimensions. Track the scores over time. Set alert thresholds for each dimension: if factual accuracy drops below 4.0, if format compliance drops below 95 percent, if the hallucination rate exceeds 3 percent. Quality monitoring catches the failures that infrastructure monitoring misses, particularly drift and degraded reasoning, which do not manifest as API errors or latency spikes but do show up as declining quality scores.

Business impact monitoring tracks the downstream effects of the AI system on business metrics. User satisfaction scores. Task completion rates. Escalation rates. Error correction rates. These are the metrics that ultimately determine whether the system is working, because a system can have good infrastructure metrics and good quality scores while still failing to deliver value to users. Business impact monitoring is the final check that ensures the technical metrics are aligned with actual outcomes.

Alerting should be tiered to match the severity of the issue. A single timeout on one request does not need an alert. A sustained increase in the fallback activation rate does. A quality score that drops below threshold on a single eval run might be noise. A quality score that drops on three consecutive runs is a trend that needs investigation. The alerting system should be tuned to avoid two failure modes: alert fatigue from too many false positives, and missed incidents from thresholds set too permissively. Both are calibration problems, and both require periodic adjustment based on operational experience.

One practice that ties monitoring and degradation together: a degradation dashboard that shows, in real time, what state each AI feature is operating in. Is the feature running on the primary model or the fallback? What is the current confidence score distribution? What is the fallback activation rate over the last hour, day, and week? What is the quality score trend? This dashboard gives the team situational awareness of the entire AI system's health at a glance. When something degrades, the dashboard shows it immediately. When everything is healthy, the dashboard confirms it. Either way, the team knows where they stand without having to investigate.

Engineering Heuristics

Heuristic 1: Every AI feature needs an explicit fallback path.

No exceptions. Before shipping any AI feature, answer the question: what does this feature do when the AI fails? If the answer is "it shows an error," the fallback path is incomplete. The answer should be a specific degradation strategy: retry, simpler model, cached response, rule-based fallback, or human escalation. Document the fallback path. Test it. Monitor its activation rate. A feature without a fallback path is a feature that will break visibly the first time the model has a bad day, and models have bad days.

Heuristic 2: Ship the fallback before you ship the feature.

Build and test the fallback path before you build the primary AI-driven path. This sounds backwards, but it is the most reliable way to ensure the fallback actually works. If you build the AI feature first and the fallback second, the fallback is always rushed, undertested, and treated as less important. If you build the fallback first, it establishes the baseline experience that the AI feature improves upon. The AI feature becomes an enhancement layer on top of a solid foundation, not a fragile primary path with a questionable safety net.

This also means the feature can ship incrementally: launch with the fallback path, validate that it works, then layer the AI on top.

Heuristic 3: A silent failure is worse than a visible one. The most dangerous AI failure is the one nobody notices. A system that confidently presents incorrect output, without any indication of uncertainty or degradation, causes damage that compounds until someone catches it. A system that says "I am not confident in this result" prevents the damage before it starts. Design your system to make failures visible: to users through confidence indicators and honest communication, and to the engineering team through monitoring and alerting. Visibility is the prerequisite for correction. Silent failures are the enemy. Make your system loud about its limitations and quiet about its capabilities, and users will trust it more than a system that does the opposite.

Chapters 9 and 10 form the evaluation pair. Chapter 9 covered how to measure quality and how to use those measurements to drive improvement. This chapter covered what to do when the measurements show a problem: degrade gracefully, keep the user experience intact, communicate honestly, and monitor continuously. Together they address the reality that probabilistic systems need different quality assurance practices than deterministic ones, and those practices need to be built into the system from the start, not bolted on when something breaks.

With Part V complete, the book has covered how to think about AI systems, how to feed them context, how to instruct them through prompts, how to govern their actions, and how to measure and handle their failures. What remains is the question of change itself. Part VI addresses the reality that everything underneath your system, the models, the providers, the capabilities, will continue to evolve, and asks how to build systems and teams that are designed for that evolution rather than disrupted by it.

Abstract Over the Model Layer

Part VI: Future

> *Tying your system directly to a specific model or provider is a liability that compounds over time. The architectural answer is abstraction: a model-agnostic interface layer that insulates your application logic from the volatility underneath it.*

This is the first of two chapters that share a single argument: the AI landscape does not reach a stable point, and software built as if it will is already accumulating technical and strategic debt. This chapter addresses the architectural response to that reality. Chapter 12 addresses the organizational and cultural response. Together they close the book with the case that adaptability is not something you add later. It is a core property of the system, designed in from the start.

Model-Agnostic Architecture

Chapter 1 argued that the model is not the product. This chapter is about the architectural implication of that argument: if the model is infrastructure, your system should be structured so that the infrastructure can be replaced without rebuilding the system.

In practice, most AI-driven applications are not structured this way. The model provider's SDK is imported directly into application code. Model-specific parameters like temperature, top-p, and token limits are hardcoded alongside business logic. Prompt templates include model-specific formatting that exploits one provider's parsing behavior. Output parsing code assumes the specific response structure of one provider's API. The model name itself appears in configuration files, service definitions, and sometimes in user-facing content.

Each of these is a coupling point. A single coupling point is easy to update. Fifty coupling points scattered across a codebase make a model migration a major engineering project. And model migrations are not hypothetical events. They are routine realities. Providers deprecate model versions. Pricing changes make a current model uneconomical. A competitor releases a model that is better for your use case at half the cost. A provider experiences reliability issues that force you to add a backup. Each of these scenarios is made dramatically easier or harder by the degree of coupling between your application logic and the specific model underneath.

Model-agnostic architecture is the practice of inserting an abstraction layer between your application logic and the model provider. The application talks to the abstraction layer. The abstraction layer talks to the provider. The application does not know or care which provider is being used. It cares about capabilities: I need a model that can summarize text, that can handle inputs of this length, that responds in this format. The abstraction layer maps those capability requirements to the specific provider and model that best satisfies them.

This is not a new pattern. It is the same principle behind database abstraction layers, cloud provider abstraction, and payment gateway interfaces. The AI-specific wrinkle is that the behavioral differences between model providers are larger than the behavioral differences between, say, database providers. Switching from one SQL database to another requires adapting a few query dialects. Switching from one model provider to another can require adapting prompts, adjusting output parsing, recalibrating confidence thresholds, and rerunning your entire eval suite. The abstraction layer does not eliminate this work, but it isolates it. The adaptation happens in the abstraction layer. The application logic stays untouched.

The objection I hear most often is that abstraction adds complexity upfront for a migration that might never happen. This objection underestimates the rate of change in the model landscape and overestimates the cost of the abstraction. A minimal abstraction layer is not expensive to build. It is an interface definition, a configuration layer, and a set of adapters. The engineering cost is measured in days, not weeks. The cost of not having it, discovered during the first migration under time pressure, is measured in weeks or months.

Let me make this tangible. A team I worked with had built their product directly on a single provider's SDK.

The provider's model was embedded in forty-three files across six services. When the provider announced a significant pricing increase, the team had ninety days to either absorb the cost or migrate. They chose to migrate. The migration took five engineers seven weeks. Not because the new provider's API was difficult, but because provider-specific assumptions were threaded throughout the codebase. Prompt templates used formatting conventions specific to the original provider. Output parsing relied on response structures unique to that provider's API. Retry logic was calibrated to that provider's specific rate limiting behavior. Token counting used that provider's tokenizer. Every one of these had to be found, understood, and adapted.

After the migration, the team spent an additional two weeks building the abstraction layer they wished they had built at the start. The total cost: nine engineer-weeks of reactive work. A team that had built the abstraction on day one would have spent two to three engineer-days on it, and the migration itself would have taken one to two weeks instead of seven. The math is not close. Building the abstraction upfront is cheaper in every scenario except the one where you never need to change providers, and that scenario is becoming less likely with every quarter that passes.

Provider Abstraction Patterns

There are several patterns for implementing provider abstraction, ranging from lightweight to comprehensive. The right choice depends on how many providers you expect to support and how frequently you expect to switch.

The adapter pattern. This is the simplest and most common approach. You define a standard interface for model interactions: a function that accepts a prompt, context, and configuration and returns a structured response. For each provider, you write an adapter that implements this interface using the provider's specific SDK and API conventions. The application code calls the standard interface. The adapter handles the translation. Switching providers means writing a new adapter and updating the configuration to point to it. The application code does not change.

The router pattern. An extension of the adapter pattern where the abstraction layer can route different requests to different providers based on criteria like cost, latency, capability, or availability. A summarization request might be routed to a cheaper model. A complex reasoning request might be routed to a more capable model. If the primary provider is experiencing latency, requests are automatically routed to a backup. The router pattern adds intelligence to the abstraction layer, turning it from a simple translation layer into an optimization layer. This is particularly valuable for teams that use multiple models for different tasks, which is increasingly common as the model landscape diversifies.

The capability-based pattern. Instead of selecting providers by name, the application specifies the capabilities it needs: text generation, code generation, image analysis, structured output. The abstraction layer maintains a registry of available providers and their capabilities, and selects the best match for each request. This is the most flexible pattern, and it maps well to a future where model capabilities are diverse and overlapping. It also makes it easy to add new providers: register their capabilities, and the system starts routing appropriate requests to them automatically.

Regardless of which pattern you choose, the abstraction layer should handle several cross-cutting concerns that differ between providers. Authentication and API key management. Rate limiting and retry logic. Request and response format translation. Error handling and error format normalization. Token counting and context window management, which varies by provider and model. Cost tracking and logging. Handling all of these in the abstraction layer means they are implemented once, consistently, rather than scattered across application code wherever a model call happens.

One practical decision that teams wrestle with: how thin should the abstraction be? The thinnest useful abstraction normalizes the API call and response format. The thickest useful abstraction also normalizes prompt formatting, output parsing, and evaluation criteria across providers. My recommendation: start thin. Normalize the call and response. Add thickness only where you encounter actual friction during a migration or a multi-provider deployment. Over-abstracting upfront leads to an abstraction layer that tries to anticipate differences that may never materialize, adding complexity without value. Under-abstracting leads to provider-specific logic leaking into application code, which is what you are trying to prevent. The middle ground is to abstract the parts that are certain to differ, the API interface and the response format, and let the rest evolve as needed.

Interface Design for Model Layers

The interface between your application logic and the model layer is the most important API in your system. It is called on every AI interaction. Its design determines how easy or hard it is to change models, add capabilities, debug issues, and monitor performance. It deserves the same design attention as your most critical public API.

A well-designed model interface has several properties.

It is prompt-centric, not provider-centric. The interface should accept a prompt (or a set of messages), configuration parameters (like maximum output length and temperature), and optional metadata (like request ID and feature name). It should not accept provider-specific parameters like model name, API version, or provider-specific formatting directives. Those details belong in the adapter, not in the interface. If the caller needs to specify a model name, the abstraction is leaking.

It returns a normalized response. Regardless of which provider handled the request, the response should have the same structure: the generated text, usage metadata (tokens consumed, latency), and any relevant quality signals (finish reason, confidence indicators). The application code should never need to check which provider responded in order to parse the response. If it does, the normalization is incomplete.

It supports structured output. Many production use cases require the model to return structured data: JSON, specific schemas, classifications from a defined set. The interface should support specifying an output schema and should handle the validation and retry logic for structured output internally. If every call site in the application implements its own JSON parsing and retry logic, that is duplicated provider-specific code that belongs in the abstraction layer.

It is observable. Every call through the interface should be logged with enough detail for debugging and monitoring: the request ID, the prompt (or a hash for privacy), the provider and model used, the latency, the token count, the response (or a summary), and any errors. This observability should be built into the interface itself, not added by each caller. Centralized logging through the interface gives you a complete picture of all model interactions in one place.

The interface should also define how errors are communicated. Model API errors, timeouts, rate limits, and content policy violations should all be translated into a consistent error format that the application code can handle uniformly. A timeout from Provider A and a timeout from Provider B should look identical to the caller. This consistency is what makes it possible to write application-level error handling once, rather than writing provider-specific error handling at every call site.

Two additional capabilities that the interface should support from the start, even if you do not use them immediately: streaming and async execution. Streaming, where the model's response is delivered token by token as it is generated rather than all at once when complete, is increasingly important for user-facing features where perceived latency matters.

Async execution, where a model request is submitted and the result is retrieved later, is important for batch processing and background tasks. Both of these have different implementation patterns across providers, and both should be normalized behind the interface so that the application code does not need to know which provider's streaming protocol or async mechanism is being used.

If these feel like details you can add later, consider that retrofitting streaming support into an interface that was designed for synchronous request-response is a significant refactor. The interface contract changes, the callers need to handle partial results, and the error handling semantics are different. Building streaming into the interface from the start, even if the first implementation does not use it, keeps the interface future-ready at negligible additional cost.

Managing Model Migrations

Even with a clean abstraction layer, switching models is not a zero-cost operation. Models differ in behavior, in quality, in how they respond to the same prompts, and in their failure modes. The abstraction layer eliminates the code-level migration cost. The behavioral migration cost remains, and it needs to be managed deliberately.

The behavioral dimension of migration is what catches teams off guard. Two models that score similarly on public benchmarks can behave very differently on your specific tasks. One model might follow instructions more literally. Another might be more creative but less consistent. One might handle long contexts well but struggle with short, precise extraction tasks. Another might excel at structured output but tend toward verbosity in open-ended generation. These behavioral differences are not bugs. They are properties of different models, and your system needs to accommodate them.

This is where the eval-first philosophy from Chapter 9 connects directly to migration readiness. If you have a comprehensive eval suite that measures the quality dimensions that matter for your specific use case, the behavioral evaluation of a candidate model is straightforward: run the eval, compare the scores, identify the gaps. If you do not have that eval suite, the behavioral evaluation is a subjective exercise of trying a few examples and guessing whether the new model is good enough. One of these approaches leads to confident, data-driven migration decisions. The other leads to costly surprises in production.

A model migration has three phases.

Phase one: evaluation. Before switching, run your full eval suite against the candidate model using your existing prompts and context pipeline. Compare the scores to your current baseline. This gives you an honest assessment of how the candidate model performs on your specific tasks, not on benchmarks or general capabilities. A model that scores higher on public benchmarks may score lower on your specific eval because your tasks have domain-specific requirements that the benchmarks do not cover. Trust your eval data over vendor claims.

Phase two: adaptation. If the candidate model scores well enough to justify migration but shows weaknesses on specific tasks, adapt your prompts. Some models respond better to different prompt structures. Some need more explicit output specifications. Some handle few-shot examples differently. The adaptation work should be isolated to the prompt layer and the abstraction layer adapters. If you find yourself modifying application logic to accommodate a new model, your abstraction layer has a gap that should be addressed.

Phase three: gradual rollout. Do not switch 100 percent of traffic to a new model at once. Use the router pattern to send a small percentage of traffic to the new model while monitoring quality metrics. Start at 5 or 10 percent. If quality holds, increase to 25, then 50, then 100. At each stage, compare the new model's production quality metrics against the baseline. If quality drops below your threshold at any stage, roll back to the previous model. This is the same canary deployment pattern used for traditional software releases, applied to the model layer.

The gradual rollout is where the eval infrastructure from Chapter 9 and the monitoring infrastructure from Chapter 10 pay off most directly. Without production quality monitoring, you are deploying a new model blind. With it, you can see, in real time, whether the new model is performing as well as the one it is replacing. The migration becomes a data-driven operation rather than a leap of faith.

One organizational practice that makes migrations smoother: schedule regular migration dry runs. Once a quarter, pick a candidate model and run it through the evaluation phase. Even if you do not intend to switch, the exercise keeps your abstraction layer honest (does it actually support a different provider without code changes?), keeps your eval suite current (does it still measure what matters?), and gives the team practice with the migration workflow. Teams that run regular dry runs handle real migrations as routine operations. Teams that have never practiced handle them as emergencies.

Vendor Lock-in Risk and Mitigation

Vendor lock-in in the AI model space is different from traditional vendor lock-in, and the differences are worth understanding because they change the mitigation strategy.

Traditional vendor lock-in is primarily about data and APIs. Migrating off a cloud provider is hard because your data is stored in their proprietary services, your code uses their specific APIs, and the switching cost grows with every new service you adopt. AI vendor lock-in shares some of these properties, you are dependent on the provider's API, pricing, and availability, but it adds a behavioral dimension. Your system's quality depends on the specific behavioral characteristics of a specific model. Prompts are tuned to how that model interprets instructions. Confidence thresholds are calibrated to that model's output distribution. Evaluation baselines are set against that model's performance. Switching models is not just a technical migration. It is a quality migration, and quality migrations are harder to manage than technical ones.

The mitigation strategy has two components: architectural mitigation, which is the abstraction layer this chapter has been describing, and operational mitigation, which is the practice of maintaining optionality.

Maintaining optionality means actively keeping your system compatible with multiple providers, even if you only use one in production. This does not mean running multiple providers simultaneously, though some teams do. It means ensuring that your prompts are written in a provider-agnostic style that works reasonably well across models, rather than exploiting model-specific behaviors that make the prompts non-portable. It means running your eval suite against at least one alternative model periodically to know how your system would perform if you needed to switch. It means avoiding provider-specific features that do not have equivalents elsewhere, or at least isolating those features behind the abstraction layer so they can be replaced.

Provider-specific features deserve special attention here, because they are the most tempting form of lock-in. A provider offers a fine-tuning service. Another offers a specialized embedding model. Another offers a unique function-calling format that is more convenient than the standard approach. Each of these is genuinely useful. Each also ties you more tightly to that specific provider. The decision to use a provider-specific feature should be made deliberately, with a clear understanding of the lock-in trade-off, and the feature should always be accessed through the abstraction layer so that a future replacement is an adapter change, not an application change.

The cost of maintaining optionality is small: a few hours per quarter to run evals against an alternative model and verify the abstraction layer still works. The cost of not maintaining optionality is discovered during the worst possible moment: when you need to switch and cannot do it quickly. A provider outage, a sudden pricing change, a deprecation notice with a short timeline. In those moments, the teams that maintained optionality switch smoothly. The teams that did not face an emergency migration with no tested alternative and no eval data to guide the transition.

There is a broader strategic point here that connects back to Chapter 1. If the model is not the product, then dependency on a specific model is a strategic vulnerability, not a strategic asset. The teams that build the best AI products treat model providers the way experienced infrastructure teams treat cloud providers: as important, valued, and replaceable partners. You invest in the relationship. You optimize for the current provider's strengths. But you do not build in a way that makes leaving impossible, because the day you need to leave will come, and you want it to be a decision you make on your terms, not a crisis you react to on theirs.

Engineering Heuristics

Heuristic 1: No model name should appear in your application logic.

This is the litmus test for abstraction. Search your codebase for model names and provider-specific identifiers. Every occurrence outside the abstraction layer and its configuration is a coupling point that will need to be changed during a migration. Model names belong in configuration files and adapter implementations. They do not belong in service logic, prompt templates, or user-facing content. If you find model names in your application code, refactor them behind the abstraction layer. This is a small investment that pays off every time the model landscape shifts.

Heuristic 2: Build the abstraction layer on day one, not migration day.

The best time to build the abstraction is when you first integrate a model. The cost is minimal: a clean interface, a single adapter, and a configuration layer. The worst time to build it is during an emergency migration, when you are simultaneously learning a new provider's API, adapting prompts, rerunning evals, and trying to ship under time pressure. The abstraction layer built on day one is clean and well-tested. The abstraction layer built during a migration is rushed and incomplete. The engineering cost is the same either way. The conditions under which you pay it are dramatically different.

Heuristic 3: Test your system against at least two model providers.

Even if you only run one provider in production, run your eval suite against a second provider at least quarterly. This practice serves three purposes. First, it verifies that your abstraction layer actually works with a different provider, not just in theory but in practice. Second, it gives you a performance baseline for an alternative, so if you need to switch, you already know how the alternative performs on your specific tasks. Third, it reveals provider-specific assumptions in your prompts and pipelines that you might not notice when testing against a single provider. These assumptions are the hidden coupling points that make migrations painful, and finding them during a routine quarterly check is far better than finding them during an emergency.

Abstraction is the architectural response to a landscape that will not stop changing. It does not predict which changes will come. It ensures that when they come, your system can adapt without being rebuilt. The abstraction layer is the structural embodiment of Chapter 1's principle: the model is not the product. What you build around the model is. And what you build around it should be designed to outlast any specific model underneath.

This chapter addressed the structural side of adaptability. The next and final chapter addresses the human side: how teams, cultures, and engineering practices can be designed to absorb continuous change rather than being disrupted by it. Chapter 12, Build for Drift, closes the book with that argument.

Build for Drift

Part VI: Future

Abstraction handles the structural problem of change. This chapter handles the human side. The engineers and teams who sustain their edge in AI are not those who learned the right tools. They are those who built habits, architectures, and team cultures designed to absorb what comes next.

Model and Capability Drift in Production

Chapter 11 addressed the deliberate changes you initiate: switching providers, migrating models, upgrading to a new version. This chapter addresses the changes that happen to you. Model behavior shifts without any action on your part. Provider capabilities expand or contract. New techniques emerge that make your current architecture suboptimal. The input distribution your system handles evolves as your user base grows and changes. None of these require you to write a single line of code, and all of them can change how your system performs.

Drift is the right word for this because it is gradual. It does not announce itself. A model provider updates their model and the quality of your summarization feature changes by two percent. Your user base shifts toward a new demographic and the distribution of inputs subtly changes. A competitor launches a new feature and your users start asking your system questions it was never designed to handle. Each individual change is small. The cumulative effect, over weeks and months, can be significant.

The insidious property of drift is that it is invisible to any monitoring system that only checks for sudden changes. A two percent quality drop in a single week does not trigger an alert. But twelve consecutive weeks of two percent drops add up to a quality degradation that users notice and that affects business metrics. By the time the degradation is visible in aggregate, it has been accumulating for months and the root cause is hard to pinpoint because there is no single event to investigate.

There are three categories of drift that production AI systems face.

Model drift. The model provider updates the model's weights, training data, or inference pipeline. The API contract stays the same. The model's name may not even change. But the behavioral characteristics shift: the model becomes more or less verbose, more or less cautious, better or worse at specific tasks. These changes are usually incremental, but they are real, and they affect systems that were tuned to the previous behavior. The prompts that produced ideal output with the old model version may produce slightly different output with the new one. Confidence calibrations that were accurate before may be off. Eval baselines that were established against the old model are no longer valid.

Capability drift. The broader AI landscape evolves, and capabilities that were cutting-edge when you built your system become baseline or even obsolete. Techniques that were impossible become straightforward. Context windows expand. Reasoning ability improves. Tool use becomes more reliable. New modalities like vision and audio become production-ready. Each of these creates an opportunity to improve your system, but only if your architecture is flexible enough to incorporate the new capability. Systems that were designed around a specific limitation, like a 4K token context window, may need significant rearchitecting to take advantage of a 200K window, even though the new capability is objectively better.

Distribution drift. The inputs your system receives change over time. New users with different needs join. Existing users adapt their behavior based on what the system does well and poorly. Seasonal patterns shift the types of queries. Product changes in other parts of your platform redirect new categories of requests to the AI system. Your eval suite, designed against the original input distribution, may not adequately cover the new distribution. Your prompts, optimized for the original use cases, may underperform on the new ones. The system is the same. The world around it moved.

The common response to all three forms of drift is the same: continuous measurement. The eval infrastructure from Chapter 9 and the monitoring infrastructure from Chapter 10 are not just tools for detecting sudden failures. They are the early warning system for gradual drift. A quality score that has been declining by a fraction of a point per week is drift. A confidence calibration that has been growing less accurate over months is drift. A fallback activation rate that has been slowly increasing is drift. If you are not measuring these metrics continuously, you will not see the drift until it has accumulated enough to cause a visible problem.

The operational response to drift depends on which category it falls into. Model drift requires re-evaluation: run your eval suite against the current model behavior, identify where quality has shifted, and adapt your prompts or confidence thresholds to the new baseline. This is the weekly behavioral regression test from the heuristics at the end of this chapter. Capability drift requires periodic architecture review: is there a new capability available that would let you simplify or improve your system? Are you still working around a limitation that no longer exists? Distribution drift requires expanding your eval dataset and possibly your prompt handling to cover the new input patterns your system is encountering.

The team-level discipline here is to treat drift as routine maintenance, not as a crisis. A team that

checks for drift weekly and makes small adjustments
treats it like changing the oil. A team that ignores drift
until quality degrades noticeably treats it like
replacing the engine. Both approaches address the
same underlying reality. One is cheaper, less
disruptive, and produces a more consistently reliable
system.

Versioning AI Behavior Over Time

Traditional software has well-established practices for
versioning. Semantic versioning communicates what
changed. Changelogs document the details.
Deployment pipelines track what is running where.
These practices exist because experience taught the
industry that knowing what changed, when, and why
is essential for operating reliable systems.

AI systems need the same discipline, but the surface
area of what needs to be versioned is broader. In
traditional software, you version the code. In AI
systems, you need to version the code, the prompts,
the context pipeline configuration, the eval datasets,
the model version, and the confidence thresholds. A
change to any of these can alter the system's behavior,

and all of them need to be tracked so that behavioral changes can be attributed to specific modifications.

The practical implementation of AI behavior versioning has several components.

A behavioral snapshot. At any point in time, you should be able to reconstruct exactly what version of every component was active: which prompt versions, which model version, which context pipeline configuration, which eval dataset, which confidence thresholds. This snapshot is the behavioral equivalent of a code release tag. When behavior changes, you compare the current snapshot against the previous one to identify what moved.

An eval history. Every eval run should be stored with its results, the behavioral snapshot it was run against, and the date. Over time, this history becomes a timeline of system quality. You can look back and see: on this date, we changed the prompt, and quality on dimension X improved by 0.3 points. On this date, the model provider updated the model, and quality on dimension Y dropped by 0.2 points. On this date, we expanded the golden dataset, and the eval became stricter, so the scores dropped even though the system behavior did not change. Without this history, quality changes are mysterious. With it, they are attributable.

A change log for AI behavior. Separate from the code changelog, a behavioral changelog documents changes that affect how the AI system behaves. Prompt modifications, context pipeline adjustments, model version changes, confidence threshold updates, eval dataset expansions. This changelog is the narrative companion to the eval history. The eval history shows what happened to quality. The behavioral changelog explains why.

Together, these components create the ability to reason about your system's behavior over time. When a stakeholder asks "why is the system responding differently than it did last month?" you can give a precise, data-backed answer. When a user reports that the system used to handle a certain type of query better, you can trace back through the history to identify what changed. When the team debates whether a recent modification was an improvement, the eval history settles the question with data rather than opinions.

This level of traceability might seem excessive, and for simple systems with a single prompt and a single model, it may be. But for any system that evolves over time, which is every production system, the traceability is what makes the evolution manageable rather than chaotic. Without it, the system's behavior is the result of an untracked accumulation of changes, and no one can explain why it does what it does. That is not engineering. That is entropy.

There is also a team health dimension to behavioral versioning. In teams without traceability, quality debates become personal. Someone changed the prompt and quality dropped, and the discussion becomes about who made the change and whether it was a good idea. In teams with traceability, quality debates are about data. The eval history shows the impact. The behavioral changelog explains the intent. The discussion becomes about whether the trade-off was worth it and what to try next. That shift, from personal blame to data-driven iteration, is one of the most valuable cultural side effects of investing in behavioral versioning. It turns quality into a team problem solved with data rather than an individual problem solved with intuition.

Staying Adaptive as a Team

The previous sections addressed architectural and process responses to drift. This section addresses the human and organizational response, because systems are built and maintained by teams, and a team's ability to adapt determines whether the architectural investments actually pay off.

The teams I have seen sustain excellence in AI engineering over multiple years share several characteristics that are worth naming explicitly, because they are not the characteristics that most hiring processes select for.

They treat learning as an operational practice, not a personal hobby. The AI landscape changes fast enough that staying current is not optional. But individual engineers reading blog posts on their own time is not a scalable learning strategy. The best teams build learning into their operational rhythm. A weekly thirty-minute session where one team member presents a new technique, paper, or tool they evaluated. A monthly review of what changed in the model landscape and whether any changes are relevant to the team's work. A quarterly review of the team's architecture against the current state of the art, asking whether any architectural decisions made six months ago should be revisited. These are not extras. They are operational practices that keep the team's knowledge current.

They run experiments regularly. Adaptive teams do not just read about new techniques. They try them. When a new prompting strategy is published, someone on the team runs it against the eval suite within a week to see if it helps. When a new model is released, someone evaluates it against the team's specific tasks, not to switch immediately but to know the option exists and how it compares. When a new tool or framework gains traction, someone builds a small prototype to assess whether it addresses a real need. The key is that experimentation is expected and supported, not something engineers have to justify or do in their spare time. A team that experiments regularly has a constantly updated map of what is possible. A team that does not is navigating with a map that is months or years out of date.

They have low attachment to their current implementation. This is the hardest characteristic to cultivate, because it runs counter to the natural pride engineers take in what they have built. An adaptive team recognizes that the prompt they spent a week perfecting might need to be rewritten when the model updates. That the context pipeline they designed three months ago might be suboptimal given a new capability. That the architecture they are proudest of might be the thing holding them back. Low attachment does not mean carelessness. It means the team evaluates their current approach on its merits, regularly, and is willing to change when the data shows a better option exists. The sunk cost of the current implementation is not a reason to keep it.

They document their decisions and the reasoning behind them. When the landscape changes and the team needs to reassess a previous decision, the quality of that reassessment depends entirely on whether anyone remembers why the decision was made. A decision documented as "we chose approach X because of constraints A, B, and C" can be revisited efficiently: are constraints A, B, and C still valid? If not, should we reconsider approach X? A decision that is not documented requires the team to reconstruct the reasoning from memory, which is unreliable, or to re-evaluate from scratch, which is wasteful. Decision documentation is the organizational equivalent of the behavioral changelog: it makes the evolution of the system's design legible and revisitable.

The Future-Proof Engineering Mindset

There is a temptation, especially in a book called "Axiom" that is built around first principles, to suggest that following these principles will make your system future-proof. That following the right practices today will protect you from whatever comes next. I want to resist that temptation, because it is misleading.

Nothing is future-proof. The AI landscape will produce surprises that no set of principles, including the ones in this book, will fully anticipate. What these principles give you is not immunity from change. They give you the capacity to respond to change efficiently. A system designed around the principles in this book is not guaranteed to survive the next paradigm shift. But it is designed to absorb it with less disruption, less rework, and less panic than a system that was not.

The future-proof engineering mindset is not about predicting the future. It is about building systems that are structurally adaptable: systems where the assumptions are explicit and testable, where the layers are separated cleanly, where the measurements are in place to detect when something changes, and where the team has the habits and practices to respond when it does.

Concretely, this mindset means accepting several things that many engineers find uncomfortable. Your system will need to change, probably sooner and more fundamentally than you expect. The model you chose is temporary. The prompts you wrote will be rewritten. The architecture you designed will evolve. The eval baselines you established will be reset. None of this means you did anything wrong. It means the landscape moved, which it will, and your system was designed to move with it.

The engineers who struggle most in this environment are the ones who treat each implementation as permanent and each change as a disruption. The engineers who thrive are the ones who treat each implementation as the current best answer and each change as an opportunity to find a better one. That is not a personality trait. It is a practice. It is the practice of investing in measurement, abstraction, documentation, and learning, so that when the ground shifts, you are not scrambling to understand what happened. You are already measuring the impact and planning the adaptation.

There are a few concrete practices that cultivate this mindset at the team level. The first is the assumption audit: once a quarter, list the assumptions your system is built on and check whether they are still valid. We assumed a 128K context window is sufficient. Is it still, or would a larger window change our architecture? We assumed structured output requires explicit JSON formatting in the prompt. Is that still true, or does the model now support native structured output? We assumed human review is necessary for customer-facing emails. Does the eval data support removing that checkpoint? Some assumptions will still hold. Others will have been invalidated by changes in the landscape. The audit surfaces the ones that need to be revisited before they cause problems.

The second practice is the explicit trade-off log. Every significant engineering decision involves trade-offs, and in AI systems, those trade-offs have a shorter shelf life than in traditional software. When the team decides to use a specific chunking strategy, they should document not just the decision but the alternative they rejected and why. When the landscape changes and someone asks "should we reconsider?" the trade-off log gives them the context to answer without re-doing the entire analysis. It also prevents the revisiting loop where the same decision gets debated repeatedly because no one remembers why it was made the first time.

Engineering Heuristics

Heuristic 1: Treat model behavior as a moving target, not a fixed dependency.

Every assumption you make about model behavior has an expiration date. The model will be updated. Its behavior will shift. The prompts you tuned against the current version will need adjustment. Design your system with this expectation built in: version your prompts, track your eval baselines, and build the infrastructure to detect and adapt to behavioral changes. A system that treats model behavior as fixed is a system that will be surprised. A system that treats model behavior as a moving target is a system that is ready for the next update.

Heuristic 2: Run periodic behavioral regression tests even without code changes.

At least weekly, run your eval suite against the production system, even if nothing in your codebase has changed. This catches model-side drift, retrieval degradation, and distribution shifts that your code-level change detection will miss. If the eval scores are stable, the run costs you nothing but compute and gives you confidence that the system is holding steady. If the scores are dropping, the run gives you early warning before users are affected. The cost of the weekly run is trivial. The cost of not running it is discovering drift weeks or months after it started, when the accumulated degradation is significant and the root cause is obscured by time.

Heuristic 3: The team that learns fastest wins, not the team with the best tools today.

In a landscape that changes quarterly, the half-life of a tool advantage is short. A team that chose the best model six months ago but has not re-evaluated since is likely behind a team that started with a weaker model but has been experimenting and iterating every month. The sustainable advantage is not what you know today. It is how quickly you can learn and integrate what you did not know yesterday. Invest in the team's learning infrastructure: regular evaluations, experimentation time, shared knowledge sessions, and documented decisions. These are the assets that compound. Specific tool choices depreciate.

Closing: What First Principles Give You

This book started with a question: in a landscape that changes as fast as AI does, what is worth building on? The answer was first principles: structural observations about how AI-driven systems behave that hold regardless of which specific models, frameworks, or providers dominate at any given moment.

Twelve chapters later, those principles have been laid out, argued for, illustrated, and made operational through engineering heuristics. Let me close by naming what they give you, collectively, as a foundation.

They give you a stable vocabulary for decisions that do not have established answers yet. When your team debates whether to give an agent access to a new tool, you can ground the discussion in the scoping frameworks from Chapter 7 and the trust levels from Chapter 8, rather than arguing from intuition. When a new model is released and the question is whether to adopt it, you can ground the decision in eval data from Chapter 9 and the migration workflow from Chapter 11, rather than reacting to hype or fear of missing out.

They give you a diagnostic framework for when things go wrong. When output quality drops, you have a systematic approach: check the context first (Chapter 4), then the prompt (Chapter 5), then the model behavior (Chapter 2), then the eval calibration (Chapter 9). When an agent misbehaves, you check the scope definition (Chapter 7), the human oversight design (Chapter 8), and the audit trail. When a migration goes poorly, you check the abstraction layer (Chapter 11) and the behavioral versioning (Chapter 12). Each principle points to a specific place to look and a specific set of questions to ask.

They give you a way to evaluate new developments on your own terms. When a new technique, tool, or model is released, you do not have to wait for someone to tell you what to think about it. You can assess it against the principles yourself. Does it improve your product layer, or does it just replace one model dependency with another? Does it respect the probabilistic nature of the system, or does it promise determinism that is not achievable? Does it compose well with your existing architecture, or does it require a monolithic redesign? Does it make your system more measurable, or does it introduce new dimensions that are hard to evaluate? The principles give you the questions. The specifics of the new development give you the answers.

And they give you durability. The specific examples in this book will age. The frameworks referenced will be superseded. The models named will be deprecated.

But the observations that the model is not the product, that context is architecture, that autonomy must be earned, that measurement drives improvement, that abstraction enables adaptation, these will hold. They will hold because they describe how a class of systems behaves, not which product to use this quarter. They are the slowest-moving layer in your decision stack, and in a landscape where everything else moves fast, that slowness is their value.

The teams that build the best AI products over the next decade will not be the ones who chose the right model at the right time. They will be the ones who built the right foundations: systems that are measured, abstracted, scoped, and designed to evolve. The right model at the right time is luck. A foundation that holds across model changes, provider shifts, and capability leaps is engineering.

That is what first principles give you. Not certainty about the future. The ability to meet it well.

The 12 Principles and Their Heuristics

This reference card summarizes the 12 principles of Axiom and the 36 engineering heuristics that make them operational. Pin it somewhere visible. Use it in design reviews, architecture discussions, and retrospectives.

#	Principle	Engineering Heuristics
1	**The Model is Not the Product**	**1.** If your differentiator is the model, you have no differentiator. **2.** Name your product layer separately from your model choice. **3.** Ask: what survives a model swap?
2	**Embrace Probabilistic Thinking**	**1.** Design for the 90th percentile, not the happy path. **2.** Never hardcode expected outputs in AI tests. **3.** Define acceptable variance before you build, not after.

3	**Context is Architecture**	**1.** Treat your system prompt like an API contract. **2.** Version your context structures the same way you version code. **3.** If the model is confused, look at the context first.
4	**Signal Over Noise**	**1.** Every token in context should earn its place. **2.** Measure retrieval quality independently from generation quality. **3.** When output quality drops, audit your context before your prompt.
5	**Prompt as Interface**	**1.** A prompt without an output spec is an incomplete interface. **2.** Write prompts for the edge case, not the average case. **3.** If you would not ship undocumented code, do not ship undocumented prompts.
6	**Composability Over Complexity**	**1.** If you cannot explain what a prompt section does in one sentence, split it. **2.** Prefer chained focused prompts over one omnibus prompt. **3.** Build a shared prompt library before writing duplicates.

7	**Scope Before Autonomy**	**1.** Start with the minimum tool surface an agent needs. **2.** Scope is a safety property, not just an organizational one. **3.** If you cannot describe what an agent cannot do, it is under-scoped.
8	**Human in the Loop**	**1.** Design human checkpoints before optimizing them away. **2.** An approval flow nobody uses is not oversight, it is theater. **3.** Log every autonomous action with enough context to reconstruct intent.
9	**Eval-First Development**	**1.** Define your success criteria before writing your first prompt. **2.** An eval suite is a product artifact, not a testing afterthought. **3.** Curate your golden dataset with the same care as your training data.
10	**Graceful Degradation**	**1.** Every AI feature needs an explicit fallback path. **2.** Ship the fallback before you ship the feature. **3.** A silent failure is worse than a visible one.

| 11 | **Abstract Over the Model Layer** | **1.** No model name should appear in your application logic. **2.** Build the abstraction layer on day one, not migration day. **3.** Test your system against at least two model providers. |
| 12 | **Build for Drift** | **1.** Treat model behavior as a moving target, not a fixed dependency. **2.** Run periodic behavioral regression tests even without code changes. **3.** The team that learns fastest wins, not the team with the best tools today. |

Decision Checklists

These checklists distill the principles into actionable decision frameworks you can use at specific moments in your development process.

Before Building an AI Feature

Define the product layer. What value does this feature deliver that is independent of which model powers it? If the answer is thin, invest in the product layer before proceeding.

Set success criteria. What does a good output look like? What does acceptable look like? What does unacceptable look like? Write these down before writing the first prompt.

Create initial golden data. Build 20 to 50 expert-labeled examples that cover typical cases, edge cases, and known-hard inputs. This is your eval foundation.

Design the fallback path. What does this feature do when the AI fails? Design and test the fallback before building the primary path.

Define acceptable variance. What is the expected accuracy? What failure rate is tolerable? What is the cost of being wrong? Document these thresholds explicitly.

Before Deploying a Prompt Change

Run the eval suite. Compare the new prompt version against the current baseline on all quality dimensions, not just the one you were targeting.

Check for regressions. Did improving one dimension degrade another? Multi-dimensional evaluation catches trade-offs that single-metric checks miss.

Review the change. Has someone other than the author reviewed the prompt change, including the reasoning for the change and the potential side effects?

Version and tag. Is the new prompt version tagged in version control? Is the eval run linked to this version? Can you roll back if needed?

Verify output parsing. If the output format changed, has the downstream parsing code been updated to match?

Before Deploying an Agent

Complete the Action Inventory. Every action the agent can take is documented with its consequences and trust level.

Write the Negative Scope Document. Every action, data source, and system the agent is prohibited from accessing is explicitly listed.

Design human checkpoints. For every Level 3 and Level 4 action, the checkpoint placement, the confirmation interface, and the escalation path are defined.

Build the audit trail. Every autonomous action is logged with input, reasoning, confidence, outcome, and reviewer identity if applicable.

Set the initial trust levels. Start conservative. Define the metrics required for each trust level promotion. Document the Progressive Expansion Plan.

Before a Model Migration

Run full eval against the candidate. Use your eval suite, not vendor benchmarks. Your tasks are what matter.

Identify adaptation needs. Which prompts need adjustment? Which confidence thresholds need recalibration? Which output parsing assumptions change?

Plan the gradual rollout. Start at 5 to 10 percent of traffic. Define quality thresholds for each escalation stage. Define rollback criteria.

Verify the abstraction layer. Can you switch models by changing configuration, or does the migration require application code changes? If the latter, fix the abstraction first.

Update the behavioral snapshot. After migration, establish new eval baselines and update the behavioral changelog.

Quarterly System Health Check

Run the assumption audit. List the assumptions the system is built on. Check whether each is still valid given the current landscape.

Run evals against an alternative model. Verify the abstraction layer works. Update the alternative model performance baseline.

Audit the context pipeline. Sample production requests and inspect the full context window. Is every piece of content earning its place?

Review the golden dataset. Are the golden outputs still correct? Does the dataset cover the current input distribution? Add recent production failures.

Check confidence calibration. Compare confidence scores against actual accuracy on a sample of recent production outputs. Adjust thresholds if calibration has drifted.

Review agent scope. Has the agent been using tools in unintended ways? Has its effective scope drifted from its designed scope? Tighten if needed.

Glossary of Key Terms

Terms as used in this book, defined for quick reference.

Abstraction layer. An interface between application logic and the model provider that isolates the application from provider-specific details. Enables model switching without application code changes. (Chapter 11)

Agent. An AI system that can take actions beyond generating text: calling APIs, reading and writing data, triggering workflows. Distinguished from a chatbot by the ability to do things, not just say things. (Chapters 7, 8)

Behavioral snapshot. A record of the exact version of every component (prompts, model, context config, eval dataset, thresholds) active at a given point in time. Used for attribution when behavior changes. (Chapter 12)

Blast radius. The worst-case consequence of an incorrect action by an agent. Used to determine the appropriate trust level and oversight for that action. (Chapter 7)

Confidence threshold. A numerical boundary that determines whether a system output is served automatically, flagged for review, or routed to a fallback. Calibrated against actual accuracy. (Chapters 2, 8, 10)

Context window. The full set of information provided to the model in a single request: system prompt, user query, retrieved documents, conversation history. The primary architectural surface of AI-driven applications. (Chapter 3)

Distribution drift. A change in the types, patterns, or characteristics of inputs a system receives over time, without any change to the system itself. Can degrade quality if the system was optimized for a previous distribution. (Chapter 12)

Eval suite. A collection of test cases, scoring rubrics, and automated scoring logic used to measure the quality of an AI system's output across defined dimensions. A product artifact, not a testing afterthought. (Chapter 9)

Fallback path. A designed degradation strategy that keeps a feature functional when the primary AI-driven path fails. Examples: retry, simpler model, cached response, rule-based fallback, human escalation. (Chapter 10)

Golden dataset. A curated collection of expert-labeled input-output pairs representing the ground truth for evaluation. The quality benchmark that the eval suite scores against. (Chapter 9)

Graceful degradation. The design practice of ensuring a system reduces capability gradually during failure rather than breaking entirely. Each degradation level preserves as much value as possible. (Chapter 10)

Hallucination. A model output that is factually incorrect but presented with the same confidence as correct information. A structural failure mode of generative AI systems. (Chapters 2, 10)

LLM-as-judge. A pattern where a language model evaluates the output of another language model, scoring it against defined criteria. Used to scale evaluation beyond what human review alone can support. (Chapter 9)

Model drift. A change in model behavior caused by provider updates to the model's weights, training data, or inference pipeline, without any change on the consumer's side. (Chapter 12)

Model layer. The component of an AI-driven application responsible for inference: sending input and receiving output from a language model. Treated as infrastructure in this book. (Chapter 1)

Negative scope document. An explicit list of actions, data, and systems that an agent is prohibited from accessing. The boundary that defines what the agent cannot do. (Chapter 7)

Product layer. Everything built around the model layer that turns a raw capability into a user-facing product: context engineering, prompt architecture, workflow integration, evaluation, guardrails. Where durable value lives. (Chapter 1)

Prompt chain. A sequence of prompts where the output of one becomes part of the input to the next. The primary mechanism for implementing modular prompt design in complex tasks. (Chapter 6)

RAG (Retrieval-Augmented Generation). An architecture where relevant documents are retrieved from an external store and included in the context window alongside the user's query, supplementing the model's internal knowledge. (Chapter 3)

Signal-to-noise ratio. The proportion of relevant to irrelevant information in the context window. Higher signal-to-noise ratio correlates with higher output quality. (Chapter 4)

Trust level. A tiered classification of agent actions by risk, determining the degree of autonomy and oversight applied. Ranges from read-only (Level 1) to autonomous consequential (Level 4). (Chapters 7, 8)

Reading Guide by Role

The book is designed to be read front to back, but different roles may want to prioritize different chapters. This guide suggests starting points based on your current responsibilities.

Backend / Platform Engineers

Start with Chapters 3 and 4 (context architecture and signal-over-noise), which address the systems you will spend the most time building. Then Chapters 11 and 5 (abstraction layer and prompt-as-interface) for the structural patterns. Return to Chapters 1 and 2 for the conceptual framing once the practical material is grounded.

Frontend / Product Engineers

Start with Chapter 10 (graceful degradation), which directly affects the user experiences you design. Then Chapters 2 and 8 (probabilistic thinking and human-in-the-loop) for the design implications of uncertainty and oversight. Chapter 5 (prompt-as-interface) is relevant if you are involved in prompt design for user-facing features.

Tech Leads / Staff Engineers

Read front to back. The architectural arguments in Chapters 1, 3, 11, and 12 are directly relevant to the decisions you make about system design and technical direction. The evaluation chapters (9 and 10) address quality infrastructure you are likely responsible for. Chapters 7 and 8 are essential if your team is building agentic features.

Engineering Managers

Start with the Introduction and Chapters 1 and 12 for the strategic framing. Then Chapters 9 and 10 (eval-first development and graceful degradation) for quality and reliability practices. Chapters 7 and 8 (agent scoping and human oversight) are essential for understanding the risk profile of agentic features your team may be building.

Data Scientists / ML Engineers Transitioning to AI Engineering

Start with Chapter 1 (the model is not the product) to reframe how you think about the role of the model. Chapters 3 and 4 (context) will be familiar in concept but different in framing. Chapter 9 (eval-first) connects to evaluation practices you already know but applies them to the product layer. Chapters 5 and 6 (prompting) address a discipline that may be newer to your background.

Tony Adesanwo

Director of Software Engineering · Match Group

Tony Adesanwo is a software engineering leader with over two decades of experience building and scaling engineering teams. As Director of Software Engineering at Match Group, he leads teams working at the intersection of product, platform, and emerging technology, with a particular focus on how AI is reshaping the way software gets designed, built, and maintained.

Over the years, Tony has worked closely with engineers navigating the disorientation of a fast-moving AI landscape, and noticed that the ones who built the best things were rarely the ones who knew the most tools. They were the ones who could reason clearly when the usual answers were not available. That observation is what Axiom is built around.

He writes and speaks on engineering leadership and AI-driven development. Axiom is his first book.

—

CONNECT

Web	tony.qodetest.com
LinkedIn	linkedin.com/in/tony-ad
Substack	fragiledev.substack.com

www.ingramcontent.com/pod-product-compliance
Lightning Source LLC
Chambersburg PA
CBHW051213130726
47988CB00001B/74